YORK

General Editors:
of Stirling) & Pro...
University of Beirut)

Oliver Goldsmith

SHE STOOPS
TO CONQUER

Notes by A. Norman Jeffares

MA PH D (DUBLIN) MA D PHIL (OXON)
Docteur de l'Universite (Lille, HC), FRSL
Professor of English Studies
University of Stirling

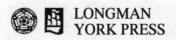

**LONGMAN
YORK PRESS**

YORK PRESS
Immeuble Esseily, Place Riad Solh, Beirut.

ADDISON WESLEY LONGMAN LIMITED
Edinburgh Gate, Harlow,
Essex CM20 2JE, England
Associated companies, branches and representatives
throughout the world

© Librairie du Liban 1980

First published 1980
Fourth impression 1996

ISBN 0 582 78226 0

Produced by Longman Singapore Publishers Pte Ltd
Printed in Singapore

Contents

Part 1

Introduction

Oliver Goldsmith

Oliver Goldsmith was born on 10 November 1728 at Pallas, near Ballymahon in the west midlands of Ireland. His father was a Protestant clergyman, generous and unworldly. It is likely that his character was the model for Dr Primrose, the vicar in Goldsmith's novel *The Vicar of Wakefield* (1766). There wasn't enough money to send Oliver to Trinity College Dublin (his father and elder brother had been educated there) as a normal undergraduate; instead he went as a sizar, a poor student, getting his education, his rooms and meals in college free in return for performing some menial tasks. Lack of money and sensitivity about his appearance – his face had been scarred by smallpox – made him unhappy. He got on badly with his tutor, indeed he ran away from the college on one occasion but was brought back by his brother, who persuaded the authorities to condone his escapade. He composed ballads, which were sung in the streets, he played the flute, and he was generous when he was in funds. He scraped through a pass degree in 1749.

After graduating Goldsmith spent nearly three years – his father had died in 1747 – at home. He tried to make his living in various ways – none of which succeeded. He was refused as a candidate for ordination; he tried being a private tutor; he attempted to emigrate but lost his money on the way to embark at Cork in the south of Ireland; he began studying law in Dublin but gambled away the money given him by his uncle. In 1752 he went to Scotland to study medicine at the University of Edinburgh.

After attending lectures at Edinburgh for two years Goldsmith moved to Holland, to follow lectures at the University of Leiden for nearly a year. Then he began his tour of Europe, walking through Flanders, France, Switzerland and Italy. He set off with 'a guinea in his pocket, one shirt to his back, and a flute in his hand'. He survived by playing the flute, and often got a fee, bed and board by disputing philosophical points publicly in universities. During his tour he learned a great deal about continental intellectual life as his essays, particularly *An Inquiry into the Present State of Polite Learning in Europe* (1759), clearly show.

He arrived in England in 1756 and tried several ways of making a living in London, as a chemist's assistant, as a proof reader for the printer (and novelist) Samuel Richardson, as a teacher in a school, and as a hack writer. He tried to obtain a post as a surgeon in India, then in 1759 he took up the hard life of literary hack work again, writing essays for various magazines. A series of *Chinese Letters* which he began to write in 1760 for the daily *Public Ledger,* published by John Newbery, was very successful. In this he took up the *persona* of a supposed Chinese philosopher visiting England and writing home about what he observed there.

By 1761 Goldsmith had been introduced to the famous author, lexicographer and conversationalist Dr Johnson (1709–84) with whom he became very friendly. His merits were appreciated by Johnson, who thought him one of the best authors of the time. Sir Joshua Reynolds, the distinguished painter, shared Johnson's high opinion of Goldsmith, and when they drew up their list of the nine original members of their famous Club they put Goldsmith's name down after their own.

Though Goldsmith was now beginning to make a reasonable living by his writing he managed his finances badly. On one occasion when he was arrested for debt Dr Johnson sent him a guinea, but when he arrived at Goldsmith's lodgings found that Goldsmith had spent the guinea on a bottle of madeira. Johnson then took the manuscript of *The Vicar of Wakefield* and sold it for sixty pounds to the publisher John Newbery; he further encouraged Goldsmith into completing his poem *The Traveller,* the first book to appear under his own name. It was well received, though many were surprised to find that he was the author. Goldsmith's own self-mockery had led some people to see him as an awkward buffoon – indeed Johnson said 'the partiality of his friends was against him'.

Newbery was well aware of Goldsmith's excellence as a writer and employed him to write Prefaces and Introductions to books as well as Histories of Rome, Greece and England. In 1769 he was engaged in writing an eight volume *History of the Earth and Animated Nature.*

In 1768 Goldsmith's first play, *The Good Natur'd Man,* had been staged, and it brought him in four hundred pounds—not a small sum at that time. Most of this he spent on entertaining his friends. He took a larger set of rooms in the Temple and Sir Joshua Reynolds painted his portrait (now in the National Portrait Gallery in London), probably in 1770, the year his second long poem, *The Deserted Village,* was published; his position as a leading author was now firmly established.

The cost, in human terms, of achieving this position had been great. Goldsmith had been overworking. He overspent when he had money, for he was over-generous to his friends and to the crowd of hangers-on who sponged on him; when in debt he would work hard and fast to repay what he owed and what he had borrowed. After he had finished his *History of England* (1771) he returned to the country to write *She Stoops to Conquer* which he finished in three months, trying, in his words, 'to do something to make people laugh'. The play was more successful than *The Good Natur'd Man*, but Goldsmith was no longer the cheerful, self-mocking man whose company his friends enjoyed; he was suffering from the strain of over-work, and he was ill, probably from kidney trouble. He was depressed, and died suddenly in April 1774.

His friends, who had not realised how serious his illness was, were saddened, and we can see why they liked him so much. Despite what Dr Johnson called his frailties, they recognised his greatness as a writer, but they also saw that, in a phrase he himself often used, there was no harm in him. He wanted to please and amuse; he took teasing well and was indeed magnanimous; he was kind-hearted and generous to a fault. As a conversationalist he was unexpected, for he used to talk to discover what he thought, having, as Dr Johnson said, no settled notions upon any subject. When he wrote, however, it was with unassuming assurance; his prose is easy to read; graceful and persuasive, it conveys his commonsense and wisdom.

The stage in the eighteenth century

A great flourishing of drama took place in England in the reigns of Queen Elizabeth the First and her successor James the First: then came a decline. The theatres were closed by the Puritan government in 1642, not to be re-opened until the Restoration of Charles the Second to the throne in 1660. The King and his courtiers enjoyed the theatre, and very many heroic tragedies and comedies of manners were written and produced successfully. This Restoration theatre existed largely in response to the aristocratic tastes of the court. Its tragedies, owing a good deal to the French theatre, portrayed a strange world where heroes attitudinised about honour, no doubt counter-balancing the cynicism and fashionable disillusion, the often cruel wit of the comedies which so frequently presented amoral characters, the rakes and libertines, who despised convention – and the ordinary citizens. There were two companies in London which provided comedies suited to a sophisticated urban audience, many of whom had come back from exile in France with a deep hatred of puritanism. They obviously enjoyed the comedies of sexual intrigue and innuendo, of smart gallants and gossiping ladies, of cuckolded old husbands, aged keepers, and young lovers resisting parental plans for marriages, of bullying fathers, of matchmaking and matching of fortunes.

The plays did not appeal to middle class audiences and disapproval of them was voiced strongly in a pamphlet written in 1698 by the Rev Jeremy Collier called *A Short View of the Immorality and Profaneness of the English Stage.* Collier attacked the plays of John Dryden (1631–1700), William Congreve (1670–1729) and John Vanburgh (1664–1726), and this attack coincided with a change in the attitudes of the audiences. Congreve's last play *The Way of the World* (1700) did not appeal to them (though it is perhaps the finest achievement of Restoration comedy), and the comedies written by George Farquhar (1677–1707) showed a shift in the way theatrical fashion was going, for Farquhar placed the action in his two best plays, *The Recruiting Officer* (1706) and *The Beaux Stratagem* (1707), outside London (in Shrewsbury and Lichfield respectively) and created characters who were less heartless than those of his predecessors. After Farquhar, writers of comedies such as the essayist and politician Sir Richard Steele (1672–1729), the actor Colley Cibber (1671–1752) and Mrs Susannah Centlivre (1667–1723) dealt with life in moral and sentimental ways – as did writers of tragedies, such as George Lillo (1693–1739). Writing for the stage became full of pathos and delicacy, even of bombast and melodrama, the lines between tragedy and comedy being particularly blurred in sentimental comedy. This now became a kind of tragedy, while tragedy itself became very domestic and trivial. Between Farquhar and Goldsmith, indeed, little drama of real merit was written, and a great deal of the comedy produced was dull.

The theatre itself was in good health as far as the skills of actors and managers was concerned. The lack of discipline often obvious in the Restoration period was no longer evident. Movable scenery, artificial lighting, and costumes were good, and the theatres were versatile. It was a period when actors and actresses became very influential in the theatre. The best of them was David Garrick (1717–49) who became a friend of Goldsmith. He adapted old plays, wrote new ones and managed the Drury Lane theatre very skilfully indeed, ensuring that the performances matched his own excellent standards of acting.

Political comment had been silenced in a Licensing Act of 1737— brought in because the corrupt government of Walpole was being effectively satirised and mocked on the stage. Through this act's provisions plays were censored by the Lord Chamberlain, and only two theatres were allowed in London, Drury Lane and Covent Garden. When Goldsmith considered the state of the theatre in his day, he was depressed by the current vogue for sentimental comedy, on which he wrote an essay in 1773. This contains his ideas about comedy, the ideas which had gone to the making of his own two comedies, *The Good Natur'd Man* (1768) and *She Stoops to Conquer* (1773). He considered sentimental comedy was undermining tragedy and removing humour from comedy by over-refining it, by making it too 'genteel'. Comedy should demonstrate humour and nature, he thought, and portray characters effectively.

Goldsmith, then, realised the need for a fresh approach. He was, however, disappointed in the reception given to his first play in 1768. *The Good Natur'd Man* upset its audiences: they hissed it as 'low' on the first night, disliking a scene where the hero, a generous but gullible man (not unlike Goldsmith himself), pretends to the heroine, Miss Richland, that the bailiffs who have arrived in his house are acquaintances of his. Goldsmith was unduly depressed, for although the play ran at Covent Garden for ten nights—quite a good run at the time—it is probable that he was upset by the fact that a sentimental play, *False Delicacy* by Hugh Kelly, which was staged at the same time at Drury Lane, was much more obviously successful.

In his first attempt at writing a play Goldsmith wasn't sufficiently skilled to rival sentimental comedy successfully, and the main reason was that he hadn't got a plot which bound the actions of the play together. His wit and irony, his characters—bashful suitor, social snob, wealthy pessimist—his situations were all fresh and lively, but they didn't cohere. *She Stoops to Conquer* shows how much he had learned by seeing *The Good Natur'd Man* on the stage. He let the audience know more about the situations of the characters on stage than they knew themselves; he placed them in a plot which contained their actions convincingly and continuously; in doing so he succeeded in his main aim of making his audiences laugh. He wrote *She Stoops to Conquer* to express his ideas about nature and human character.

Goldsmith and another Irish author, Richard Brinsley Sheridan (1751–1816), author of *The Rivals* (1775) and *The School for Scandal* (1777), enlivened the theatre in the 1770s and their plays have continued to hold the stage because they are in the line of great comedy: pruning excesses, developing the ironies of situations, letting the audience know more about the characters than they know themselves. These plays are filled with a mixture of humour and farce, with amusing situations, and with lively, indeed often sparkling dialogue. After them no comedies of any lasting merit were written for the stage until two more Irish dramatists, Oscar Wilde (1854–1900) and George Bernard Shaw (1856–1950) revitalised the classic concept of comedy again in the latter part of the nineteenth century.

A note on the text

The first edition of *She Stoops to Conquer, or The Mistakes of a Night* was printed for Francis Newbery in 1773. It is available in many editions, the present Notes using the text in the MacMillan English Classics series, edited A. Norman Jeffares, MacMillan, London, 1965. That edition is based on the first edition of the play, but its editor has modernised Goldsmith's spelling and punctuation.

Part 2

Summaries
of SHE STOOPS TO CONQUER

A general summary

The play opens by showing us Mr and Mrs Hardcastle, who live in the country, discussing her son by her first marriage, Tony Lumpkin, who is a wild young man full of high spirits. Kate Hardcastle, the daughter of the house, is told by her father that he expects a visit from young Marlow, the son of his friend Sir Charles Marlow, whom he has chosen to be Kate's husband. Kate tells her friend Constance Neville, who is a niece of Mrs Hardcastle, about Marlow, who turns out to be a close friend of Constance's admirer, Mr Hastings. Constance describes Marlow to Kate as very modest among virtuous women, but with a different character 'among creatures of another stamp'. We also learn that Mrs Hardcastle hopes that Constance—who has a fortune—will marry her son Tony Lumpkin. Constance pretends to Mrs Hardcastle that she is in love with Tony (who doesn't want to marry her) so that her real attachment to Hastings can remain secret, since Mrs Hardcastle has the management of Constance's fortune.

The second scene of the first act is set in an alehouse, where Tony is singing. When the landlord brings in Marlow and Hastings, who have lost their way, Tony informs them it's too far to Mr Hardcastle's house, and then directs them there, telling them that it is an Inn with an Innkeeper who wants to be thought of as a gentleman.

In the second act the two young men arrive at the Hardcastles' house, thinking it an Inn, and we learn that Marlow has really come to the country to aid Hastings, who is not interested in Constance's fortune, but wants to marry her; the Hardcastle family don't know Hastings, so Marlow can introduce him as his friend. When Mr Hardcastle arrives to greet them they treat him as an Innkeeper. Having heard of Marlow's modesty, Hardcastle is amazed by the way the young men interrupt him and demand to discuss the bill of fare for dinner.

When Hardcastle shows Marlow to his room Constance meets Hastings and she tells him of their mistake. Hastings intends to take her to France to be married as soon as the horses are refreshed after the journey. She has been persuading her aunt to let her wear the jewels which make up her fortune, and thinks she has nearly succeeded. He tells her he's not interested in her fortune but persuades her not to tell Marlow about their mistaking the house for an Inn; because of

Marlow's strange character, Hastings says, he might leave the house before their plan to elope is ready to be executed. Marlow enters and Hastings introduces him to Constance, telling him that Constance and Kate have called at the Inn on their way home. Marlow is confused, but persuaded to stay and meet Kate. He makes some shy, lame, awkward remarks to her before leaving. She thinks him an odd young man, but one with possibilities.

There follows a scene where Hastings gets on well with Mrs Hardcastle and Tony exhibits his reluctance to obey his mother's behests. After Mrs Hardcastle and Constance depart, Tony, when he hears that Hastings proposes to take Constance off to France, is delighted, and promises to help them by providing horses and maybe getting them part of Constance's fortune in jewels.

The third act opens with Hardcastle and Kate, who has changed her dress, exchanging their different views of Marlow, he regarding him as a bouncing swaggering puppy, she seeing him as timid, awkward, bashful. They agree to reject him, then decide to wait, to see if the contradictions in Marlow can be reconciled.

Tony gives Hastings Constance's jewels which he has stolen from his mother's bureau, but Hastings is worried because he knows Constance is trying to persuade Mrs Hardcastle to give them to her. When Hastings leaves, Mrs Hardcastle and Constance enter, and Constance hears the jewels are missing, and is offered Mrs Hardcastle's garnets. When Mrs Hardcastle goes off to get them, Tony tells Constance that Hastings has got the jewels; but Mrs Hardcastle returns proclaiming the theft. She and Tony exit, arguing furiously. He had suggested earlier that his mother should tell Constance the jewels were missing, and he now pretends his mother *is* pretending they are.

Next we hear from Kate's maid that Marlow has seen Kate passing by and, not recognising her in her changed dress, thinks she is the barmaid. Kate then pretends to be the barmaid, to see what Marlow is really like. When he arrives, he flirts outrageously with her and is embracing her when Mr Hardcastle appears. Marlow leaves hastily and Kate says that she will convince her father that Marlow *is* modest. Mr Hardcastle, however, is about to turn Marlow out of the house, but she begs for an hour to convince him she is right, to which he agrees.

The tempo speeds up in the fourth act when Hastings hears from Constance that Sir Charles Marlow's arrival is imminent. Hastings tells her that they must complete their plans before he comes, because he knows Hastings, and will tell Mr Hardcastle who he is. Hastings reassures Constance that the jewels are safe because he has sent them to Marlow, and she says she'll pretend to her aunt that she has a violent passion for Tony.

Marlow, however, has unwittingly upset Hastings's plan because he has given the casket to the supposed landlady, Mrs Hardcastle, to keep safely. When he enters he tells Hastings that he is getting on well with the barmaid, and then Hastings learns from him that the jewels are in Mrs Hardcastle's keeping again. Without telling Marlow, Hastings decides that Constance and he must set off without any hope of obtaining her fortune.

Marlow next tells Mr Hardcastle that he has ordered his servants to drink freely. Hardcastle orders him to leave, whereupon Marlow gets in a fury and demands his bill. Hardcastle's remarks as he leaves stir doubts in Marlow, who begins to wonder if he really is in an Inn. When Kate enters he asks her if it is. She replies that it is Mr Hardcastle's house, in which she is a poor relation; and then she weeps because he says he must never show his face in the house again. He is touched by her regard for him and leaves the room, regretting that he cannot follow his own inclinations. Kate decides that she will not let him go and will tell her father about her having pretended to be the barmaid.

Tony tells Constance that he has horses ready for the elopement but that they must pretend to be courting to deceive his mother. She enters, persuaded the jewels were mislaid by a mistake of the servants, and, seeing them fondling each other, promises Constance the jewels and says they'll be married next day. A note is brought in for Tony, who can't read well, so Constance, realising it is from Hastings, pretends to read it, saying it is about cock fighting, but Tony gives his mother the letter to read, and she then discovers that Hastings is waiting for Constance at the bottom of the garden, that he hopes Tony will provide fresh horses for them to get away.

Mrs Hardcastle is furious and decides to take Constance off to stay with another aunt who will keep her secure. She leaves, telling Tony to be ready to accompany her, and Hastings then enters, raging because he has been betrayed by Tony's giving the note to his mother to read; next Marlow comes in, furious that he has been made a fool of; the two young men and Constance turn on Tony, but the scene ends with Tony promising to alter things; he says they should meet him at the bottom of the garden in two hours' time.

The final act opens with Hastings learning from a servant that Mrs Hardcastle and Constance have gone off in a post-coach with Tony in attendance on horseback. Sir Charles Marlow has arrived, and he and Hardcastle laugh over Marlow's mistake, deciding that, as the couple like each other (as Kate has told her father), they can marry. But Marlow when he enters denies that he is interested in Miss Hardcastle, says he met her once and that formally. He hopes he may be allowed to leave a house in which he has been so mortified. After he leaves, Kate says to her father and Sir Charles Marlow that young

Marlow *has* seen her several times and professed love for her. His father is baffled; but he and Mr Hardcastle agree to Kate's suggestion that they hide behind a screen in half an hour when she says they'll hear Marlow declare his passion to her.

At the back of the garden Hastings is joined by Tony, who tells him he has brought the coach back by a circuitous route and lodged it in the horse pond at the bottom of the garden. Hastings, he says, can put his own horses to the coach and elope with Constance, since the other horses are exhausted and thus no one can follow them. Mrs Hardcastle then enters, thinking she is forty miles from home. Next Hardcastle comes on stage, and Tony tries to pretend to him that he has come back alone. Mrs Hardcastle thinks Tony is talking to a highwayman, but Hardcastle in some perplexity assures her that she is at home. She follows Tony off stage in a rage. Constance then tells Hastings that she has decided not to run away but to appeal to Mr Hardcastle.

In the third scene Marlow declares to Kate, whom he still thinks to be a poor relation of the Hardcastles, that he is not so interested in getting a fortune, that he will stay, and that his father will approve of her. The two fathers interrupt this declaration, and he learns his mistake. Kate mocks him by repeating some of his earlier remarks to her when he thought her a barmaid. He tries to go, but they assure him Kate will forgive him.

After Mrs Hardcastle enters Sir Charles tells them Hastings is a good, worthy man: it is clear that, if Tony doesn't want to marry Constance when he comes of age, she can have her fortune. Hastings and Constance enter, and plead for understanding. Tony, at his stepfather's instigation, refuses Constance's hand and Hardcastle discloses that Tony has been of age for three months. Tony then formally refuses her again, and so Constance and Hastings can marry, and Kate agrees to marry Marlow. All is well, and, as Hardcastle remarks, the mistakes of the night are over.

Detailed summaries

The Dedication

NOTES AND GLOSSARY:

Samuel Johnson, LLD: Dr Johnson (1709–84) was a good friend to Goldsmith. He was a lexicographer, poet, critic, journalist, and conversationalist. His *Life,* written by his friend James Boswell, records his unusual character

particularly . . . partiality: because Johnson had been instrumental in persuading George Colman who managed the Covent Garden theatre to produce *She Stoops to Conquer.* Colman was reluctant to do so (and two of the actors refused to take part in it)

comedy . . . not merely sentimental: sentimental comedy was popular at the time; in it virtue triumphed over vice. Goldsmith wrote an essay condemning it in 1773

dangerous . . . Mr Colman . . . various stages: Colman finally decided to take the play only when Goldsmith brought it to David Garrick to consider for the rival Drury Lane theatre

late in the season: the season closed on 31 May; the play was produced in March, but there were only twelve occasions on which it could be performed, because of holidays, and nights when performances were given for the benefit of the actors

Dramatis Personae

This gives the names of the actors and actresses who played in the first performance of the play.

NOTES AND GLOSSARY:

Dramatis Personae: *(Latin)* the characters in the play

Mr Lewes: Goldsmith wrote an Epilogue to the play when a benefit performance for this actor, Charles Lewes, was staged on 17 May 1773

Mr Quick: on 8 May 1773, a benefit performance was staged for John Quick, who had acted as the Post-boy in Goldsmith's *The Good Natur'd Man*

Mrs Green: this actress had also played in *The Good Natur'd Man,* as Garnet. A benefit performance was given for her on 3 May 1773

Mrs Bulkley: an actress who played Miss Richland in *The Good Natur'd Man*. She couldn't sing, so the song 'Ah me! When shall I marry me' had to be omitted from *She Stoops to Conquer*

The Prologue

In this Prologue Garrick indicates that there may be a change in public taste away from sententious, sentimental comedy. The actor Woodward who speaks the prologue indicates the sick state of true comedy; if true comedy dies, then she will be succeeded by a worthless woman fond of sentimentality. Woodward wonders what will become of him and his fellow actor Ned Shuter if true comedy vanishes. He tries to act in the style of sentimental comedy, but gives up, saying 'morals' [moralising] won't do for him. There is only one hope, that if the audience swallows the Doctor's [Goldsmith's] remedy, comedy will be cured. The audience are like a college of Physicians whose applause will convey a degree upon the dramatist-doctor.

NOTES AND GLOSSARY:

David Garrick: Garrick (1717–79) was a brilliant actor, and was manager of the Drury Lane theatre from 1747; he was a friend of Johnson and Goldsmith, and a member of Johnson's famous Literary Club

Mr Woodward: Edward Woodward was known as a comic actor; he played Lofty in Goldsmith's *The Good Natur'd Man,* but had refused the role of Tony Lumpkin in *She Stoops to Conquer*

'Tis not alone . . . I've that within': this is an adaption of Shakespeare, *Hamlet,* I. 2: 'Tis not alone my inky cloak, good mother . . . That can denote me truly . . . But I have that within which passeth show'

The Comic Muse: Thalia who was the muse of comedy and pastoral poetry. In Greek mythology there were nine muses, the daughters of Zeus and Mnemosyne

player: an actor

Shuter . . . Poor Ned: Edward (Ned) Shuter played the part of Mr Hardcastle; he had played Croaker in *The Good Natur'd Man*

a mawkish drab . . . sentimentals: a worthless woman who is fond of sentimentality

be moral: act in a moralising manner typical of sentimental comedy

All is not gold . . . stumble: taken from *The Hind and the Panther* (1685) a religious satirical poem by John Dryden (1631–1700). The sentences that follow are sententious moral maxims

morals: moral maxims or reflections

A Doctor: Goldsmith held the degree of Bachelor of Medicine, and had for one brief period of his life practised medicine. Here he is attending the Muse of comedy who is desperately ill

Five Draughts: five doses, the five acts of the play

the maid: the Muse of (true) comedy

The College, you: You, the audience, are like a College of Physicians or Surgeons

Regular . . . Quack: the audience by its applause can confer a degree upon the dramatist-doctor, thus making him Regular, or fully qualified; if not, he will be called a quack, an untrained amateur

---

Act 1 Scene 1

In the first scene Goldsmith shows us very efficiently the nature of some of the characters in the play. Mrs Hardcastle would like to go to London but her husband is against change; he likes what is old. They live in an old, out of the way house which Mrs Hardcastle says is like an inn (thus we are prepared for the subsequent mistake); they don't have company (which explains the special preparations made to receive the visitors later); we are told of their ages; that Tony Lumpkin is Mrs Hardcastle's son by her first husband; that they disagree about his habit of practical joking. When he enters he shows his interest in the local alehouse and when he leaves with his mother we see how she dotes on him.

Kate, daughter of the Hardcastles, is a different kind of person; she seems obedient – to please her father's desire for simplicity, she wears a housewife's dress in the evenings, though she dresses as she pleases in the mornings. (This fact helps to make her seem like a bar-maid to Marlow later in the play.) Hardcastle tells her he has invited an eligible young man from town to stay, whom he intends she shall marry. Kate demurs, since she doesn't know him, but Hardcastle says he won't control her choice. He disappears to prepare the servants to receive Marlow. She is excited by this news; she likes the description of him as young and handsome; but while she approves of his being sensible and good-natured, she doesn't like his being reserved and sheepish.

She tells her friend Constance Neville, who is a niece of Mrs

Hardcastle, of the promised arrival of Marlow and hears he is a close friend of Hastings, who is Constance's secret admirer. Constance tells her Marlow is modest among women of virtue but very different with other kinds of women. Constance has been seeing Mrs Hardcastle, who wants her to marry Tony. The management of Constance's fortune – it consists largely of jewels – is in Mrs Hardcastle's hands, and Constance pretends she likes Tony, to conceal her love for Hastings. Tony doesn't want to marry her. This scene shows us that there are complications; people are not what they seem. Marlow is not as modest as he may seem in polite company, and Tony is better natured than he may seem. Mrs Hardcastle doesn't realise Constance is not in love with her son and is hoping to marry Hastings.

NOTES AND GLOSSARY:

to town: to the capital, London

Misses Hoggs . . . Mrs Grigsby: rustic names, suggesting insignificant people. Hogg suggests pig; a grig is a small person or creature

fopperies: affectations

inside passengers . . . basket: ladies and gentlemen travelled in the inside part of a coach; the basket, a large boot at the rear, was intended for luggage, or could be used by servants and outside passengers paying a cheap rate. Hardcastle implies that the outside passengers and servants are as affectedly fashionable as the ladies and gentlemen inside a coach

Oddfish . . . Cripplegate: the names are somewhat derogatory

Prince Eugene: an Austrian General (1663–1736). He fought against the Turks with distinction in the 1690s; he fought against the French with the Duke of Marlborough in the reign of Queen Anne

Duke of Marlborough: John Churchill (1650–1722) first Duke of Marlborough, an English General, who commanded the forces of the Grand Alliance from 1702–11, winning the Battle of Blenheim in 1711. He was dismissed from office in 1711. His great house, Blenheim Castle, near Woodstock in Oxfordshire, was built for him by the nation; it was designed by John Vanburgh, the architect and dramatist ·

trumpery: trifles; something of less value than it seems

Darby . . . Joan: a devoted couple who lived in Yorkshire in the eighteenth century. Their happiness was celebrated in a ballad attributed to Matthew Prior (1664–1721), but probably written by Henry Woodfall

twenty to twenty: Mrs Hardcastle is saying that she is forty years old

make money of that: see what good you get out of it; the equivalent of the phrase 'put that in your pipe and smoke it'

fifty seven . . . twenty: Hardcastle says that she is fifty-seven, but she argues that she was twenty when her son Tony was born and he has not yet come to years of discretion (that is, come of age, at twenty-one). Hardcastle is teasing his wife: if he were right, Tony would be thirty-seven. We are told a little further on that he has not yet got his inheritance of fifteen hundred pounds a year from his dead father's estate, and at the end of the play we hear that Mrs Hardcastle has kept his exact age from him; Hardcastle has agreed to this because it might conduce to Tony's improvement if he did not know he was twenty-one and independent

quotha: said he. This is used in a contemptuous way, as if 'indeed' were used after the repetition of a word or phrase employed by another

fastened my wig: Lord Clare's daughter once played this trick on Goldsmith

A cat and fiddle: nonsense

The Three Pigeons: the name of the local alehouse. After the play the local inn at Lissoy, where Goldsmith grew up in Ireland, was called by this name

exciseman: an official who prevented smuggling and collected duty on imported goods

Little Aminadab: Aminadab was originally a slang term for a Quaker

music box: a mechanical instrument, consisting of a revolving toothed cylinder working upon a resonant comb-like metal plate

Gauze: transparent material

French frippery: frippery is cheap finery

housewife's dress: the fact that she uses this plain dress later in the play leads to Marlow's thinking her the barmaid

recruits . . . muster: they are as untrained as recruits on the first day they enlist

anything whimsical about me?: Do I look odd?

Am I in face today?: Do I look my best?

tête-à-têtes: (from the *French*, literally 'head-to-head') conversations between two people

pink of perfection: in the eighteenth century pink meant 'the best type of' or 'highest'. In the Elizabethan period pink often meant a flower

improvements:	alterations to the house or garden or grounds. There was a fashion for making estates picturesque either by regularity or by a planned wildness (called Sharawadgi in imitation of the Chinese fashion)
Allons!:	*(French)* Let's go

would it were bed-time: said by Falstaff, in Shakespeare's *Henry IV, Part I* (V.1.125) on the eve of the Battle of Shrewsbury

---

Act 1 Scene 2

This scene contains the basis of the plot, Tony Lumpkin's practical joke in which he sends Marlow and Hastings to his step-father's house under the impression it is an inn. Tony is happy in the Three Pigeons, the local tavern; he sings a song, and is popular because he takes after his father. He is thinking of Bett Bouncer, he says; and he is paying for the drinks. The landlord tells him that two gentlemen have lost their way, and Tony realises that one of them must be the gentleman who is coming to court his sister. He clears out the rustics, and, when Marlow and Hastings arrive, tells them that Mr Hardcastle's house is too far away for them to reach it that night. The landlord says the inn is full up, and Tony suggests that they should go to the Buck's Head, a mile away. The landlord protests to Tony at his sending them to his father's house but is told to keep quiet, while Tony informs the young men that the landlord is about to give up business, and, as he wants to be considered a gentleman, is inclined to give his company to his guests. Tony says he'll show them on their way.

NOTES AND GLOSSARY

knock himself down for a song:	Tony is acting as master of ceremonies, knocking down with his mallet (like a toastmaster at a dinner) those whom he calls on to speak or sing
genus:	*(Latin)* race, the human race
Lethes . . . Styxes . . . Stygians:	in Greek mythology, Lethe was the river of forgetfulness, the Styx the river of hate in the underworld over which the shades of the dead were ferried by Charon, and by which the Gods swore their most solemn oaths. Stygian is the adjective pertaining to the river Styx or the infernal regions, meaning black or gloomy
Quis . . . Quaes . . . Quods:	*(Latin)* relative pronouns, meaning who and which

Methodist preachers: Methodism developed as a reaction against the Anglican Church of England; the name was applied to the Oxford Society of pious young men which Charles Wesley (1707–88) founded, and to which his brother John (1703–91) and George Whitefield (1714–70) belonged. Methodist or Wesleyan preachers held meetings all over the country and their emotional preaching had a powerful effect

skinful: bellyful

the pigeon: the dupe

jorum: a large drinking vessel, usually used for drinking punch; it could also mean the contents of the vessel

bustard: a large game bird

widgeons: a species of wild duck

nothing that's low: Goldsmith here is attacking the conventions of contemporary drama by putting them in the mouths of rustics. A scene of his own first play *The Good Natur'd Man* was considered low (see p.7)

concatenation: a chain of events, or of thoughts

maxum: maxim

to dance a bear: he has to make his living by being in charge of a dancing bear

'Water Parted': a song from an opera *Artaxerxes* (1782) by Thomas Augustin Arne (1710–78) the English composer

the Minuet: this follows the overture in *Ariadne* an opera by George Frederick Handel (1685–1759)

winding the straight horn: blowing a hunting horn

pay no reckoning: don't pay the bill

Stingo: a strong drink, here a nickname for the landlord of the Three Pigeons

post-chaise: a travelling horse-drawn carriage

woundily: extremely

grumbletonian: grumbler. Originally it was used as a nickname for the country party (as opposed to the Court party) in the reign of William and Mary

unaccountable reserve: notice that Marlow's unusual character is being emphasised

we wanted no ghost to tell us that: in other words, its obvious. The phrase comes from Shakespeare's *Hamlet,* (I.5): There needs no ghost, my lord, come from the grave To tell us this

trapesing: flaunting

trolloping: untidy, slovenly

Zounds:	an abbreviation of the oath 'By God's wounds'
longitude:	in 1714 a reward was offered by Parliament for an accurate means of discovering longitude; it was won by John Harrison. He finally got the money in 1773 (the year *She Stoops to Conquer* was performed) as the king intervened on his behalf

sending them to your father's as an inn: technically Mr Hardcastle is Tony's stepfather. This trick of misdirection was played on Goldsmith himself when he was young

his mother . . . alderman, and his aunt . . . justice of peace: Tony is saying that Hardcastle will boast of his relatives

blade:	he is a dashing old man; wearing a sword indicates the nature of his character

---

Act 2 Scene 1

Hardcastle drills his servants, who are unused to his having guests in the house. He finds it difficult to get them to see how to act as normal, well-trained servants.

Marlow and Hastings come in and discuss inns. Again we hear of Marlow's shyness with modest women; he has come down to the country partly to please his father, and doesn't expect to make much impression on Kate; his chief inducement, however, has been to aid Hastings in his plan to marry Constance Nevill. Hastings tells Marlow that she wants to marry him, that her deceased father agreed to this, and that he isn't seeking to carry off a fortune.

Hardcastle greets them, but they ignore his attempts to make conversation, telling them anecdotes of his military service. Marlow interrupts him to ask for a glass of punch, and they agree to humour him, thinking him an unusual character. He again reverts to his military experiences and Marlow again interrupts him to ask what is for supper. He asks for the cook, and when Hardcastle demurs, demands the list of what is in the larder. The young men discuss the bill of fare and think it too complicated; then Marlow insists on seeing that the beds are properly aired. Hardcastle thinks this insistence impudent, but goes with him.

Hastings, who stays behind, thinks the supposed landlord's civilities are troublesome. Then he is delighted to find Constance, who tells him that the house is not an inn at all but that her aunt and guardian, Mrs Hardcastle, lives in it. She realises Tony must have tricked them and tells Hastings that he has nothing to fear from Tony Lumpkin, but that her aunt hopes she will marry him. Once the horses have recovered from their journey Hastings aims to take Constance to France where they can be married. She wants to wait till she gains possession of her fortune which is in jewels. She is trying to persuade her aunt to let her wear them. Hastings says he isn't interested in the jewels, but that Marlow musn't be told about their having mistaken the house for an inn, as he might leave before they could manage to carry out their plan of eloping.

Marlow enters, to be told by Hastings, on his return, that Constance Neville and Kate Hardcastle have called at the inn to get fresh horses. Marlow tries to leave but Constance persuades him to stay, saying Kate knows he is in the house. When Kate arrives Marlow is very awkward and uneasy in his halting conversation with her. Hastings and Constance leave Marlow alone with Kate and he continues for a time to falter bashfully through various remarks. Kate thinks that despite this sober interview, broken off by Constance calling them, Marlow has good sense – if she could only teach him to have confidence in himself.

Tony and Constance then enter, followed by Hastings and Mrs Hardcastle, who is greatly taken by his talk of London, which she only knows at second hand. He pays her compliments and she tells him that Constance and Tony are contracted to each other. Tony makes it clear that he doesn't care for Constance but Mrs Hardcastle refuses to see this; however, when he demands to be given his fortune she calls him provoking, saying she never sees him when he's in spirits.

When Mrs Hardcastle and Constance leave, Hastings praises Constance to Tony, but Tony is highly critical of her, saying she doesn't compare with Bet Bouncer, whereupon Hastings tells him he plans, if Tony will help him, to elope to France with Constance – a plan which pleases Tony, who promises to get Hastings a fresh pair of horses for the chaise, and thinks that he may also get the lovers part of Constance's fortune, the jewels.

NOTES AND GLOSSARY:

Militia: an auxiliary branch of the British army, distinct from the regular army

yeating: supposed dialect, eating

Ecod: variant of Egad, 'by God!' used as a mild oath

upo' upon

bauld: supposed dialect, bold

pleace: supposed dialect, place

cartain: supposed dialect, certain

wauns: supposed dialect, wounds, elliptical for 'God's wounds', an oath

canna: cannot

numskulls: people with skulls too thick to feel anything, stupid people

By the elevens: probably by the eleven apostles (excluding Judas who betrayed Jesus Christ)

I'ze: supposed dialect, I'll

inflame a reckoning: increase the bill. This echoes *The Two Noble Kinsman* by John Fletcher (1579–1625), probably in association with Shakespeare, (III.5.130): informs the tapster to inflame the reck'ning

college bed-maker: women who acted as servants in residential colleges

a comet: a comet had appeared in 1769

a burning mountain: Vesuvius in Italy erupted in 1767

bagatelle: *(French)* a trifle

courted by proxy: arranged marriages were common in the medieval and renaissance periods and even later. The bridegroom and bride might well not see each other before the day of their marriage

prepossessing: biasing, or causing prejudice; here the meaning is unprepossessing, as 'awkward' indicates

'prentice: apprentice

duchesses of Drury Lane: women of low repute; the reputation of Drury Lane and its neighbourhood was disreputable at this time

the white and gold: his white and gold suit

This is Liberty-hall: this echoes a remark (*hi sunt liberae aedes:* This is Liberty Hall) made by the character Pleusicles in the *Miles Gloriosus*, a famous Latin comedy by Plautus (250–184BC)

Denain: the French under Marshall Villars defeated the allies there in 1712. The Duke of Marlborough had been dismissed the year before. So Hardcastle (or Goldsmith) is getting his facts wrong

ventre d'or: *(French)* goldfronted

George Brooks: probably an imaginery character

Here's cup: a drink made up of some alcoholic liqour – claret or cider probably, flavoured with fruits and herbs

mistakes of government: the government of Lord North (1732–79) was not efficient; it was in difficulties in the North American Colonies and in India

Heyder Ally: Heyder Ally, Sultan of Mysore, South India (1761–82) who made his own terms with the government of Madras

Ally Cawn: Ali Khan was Nawab of Bengal from 1760–64. After the Battle of Buxar in 1764 he fled from Bengal, of which Warren Hastings became Governor in 1772

Ally Croaker: an Irishman in a comic song, popular about twenty years before Goldsmith wrote *She Stoops to Conquer*

The Battle of Belgrade: a battle of 1717 in which Prince Eugene (the war against the Turks resumed in 1716) defeated a large Turkish army and took Belgrade

Westminster Hall: the site of the Law Courts in London until 1882

Colonel Wallop: probably another invented name

Joiners' company . . . Corporation of Bedford: one of the London guilds. or professional associations. This one had a reputation for eating and dining particularly well, as had the Town Corporations (or governing bodies) such as Bedford

Florentine: a baked dish, containing minced meat, eggs, currants and spices

a shaking pudding: a jelly

a taffety cream: a dish made of cream thickened so that it looked like taffeta silk, thin and lustrous

a green and yellow dinner: where highly coloured plates and decorations hardly compensate for inadequate food

even among slaves: the French were often alluded to as slaves before the French Revolution of 1789

the India Director: a director of the East India company and consequently a wealthy man

perish the baubles: don't bother about the jewels

insure: guarantee

Cicero: Marcus Tullius Cicero (106–43BC) the famous Roman orator, statesman and man of letters

a man of sentiment: a man of good breeding

sentimental: refined

Ranelagh, St James's, or Tower Wharf: Ranelagh and St James's were fashionable areas of London (The King lived at St James's Palace), but Hastings is mocking Mrs Hardcastle's ignorance of London when he adds in Tower Wharf, which was the resort of thieves and fisherwomen

the Pantheon, the Grotto Gardens, the Borough: here Mrs Hardcastle herself demonstrates that she knows nothing about life in London. She mixes up the Pantheon, a teahouse in Oxford Street, and the Grotto Garden, (probably Vauxhall Gardens) which were fashionable resorts, with the Borough, where Southwark Fair, a disreputable affair, was held. It was not a place to which ladies would have gone

tête-à-tête . . . the Scandalous Magazine: this is *The Town and Country Magazine* which contained gossip and scandal. It also published *tête-à-tête* portraits of people (who didn't know each other)

Miss Rickets of Crooked Lane: country ladies frequently wrote to a correspondent in London for dress materials and news of the fashions. Crooked Lane is in the City of London; and the disease of rickets results in crooked, malformed limbs

degagee: *(French)* nonchalant

Friseur: *(French)* hairdresser

such a head: such a way of dressing the hair

Lady May'ress: the wife of the Lord Mayor of London

City Ball: in the city of London

inoculation: inoculation was introduced into England in 1721 from Turkey by Lady Mary Wortley Montagu (1689–1762), who was the wife of the British Ambassador at Constantinople. By about 1740 it was generally accepted as a good measure against smallpox. Jenner's system of vaccination was discovered in 1799. Before inoculation many people were disfigured by the pock marks left by the disease, Goldsmith himself having suffered thus; he contracted the illness as a child

single button: the current fashion was for short waistcoats with fewer buttons. Mr Hardcastle likes old fashions, so he continues to wear a long waistcoat

flaxen wig: small wigs were becoming fashionable and some men were wearing their own hair

Gothic: barbarous, uncouth

tête: *(French)* here a head of false hair, a wig

samplers: needlework, usually worked in cross-stitch; they usually portrayed a motto or text, and were decorated with patterns of animals, trees and geometric designs. Usually they were made by girls

Mrs Niece: 'Mrs' applied to young girls usually implied disapproval though the title when given to elderly maiden ladies was a sign of respect

Ecod!: another form of the mild oath 'Egad'

before faces: in front of people, in public

crack: this may mean a lie, or else it may be Tony cracking his whip

The Blenkinsop mouth: presumably Blenkinsop is a name in her family

(measuring):	a stage direction. They are standing back to back
O lud:	O Lord
fortin:	fortune
receipt:	recipe

The Complete Huswife: a popular eighteenth-century handbook which contained recipes, medical advice and miscellaneous information

coursing me through Quincy: giving him medical remedies or tonics prescribed by John Quincy (*d.*1723)

the first day's breaking: the first day of training a young horse

as loud as a hog: as noisy as a hog stuck in a gate

Bandbox: her beauty comes out of her bandbox, meaning she is made-up. Tony explains what he means in the next sentence calling Constance 'a made-up thing'

Anon: usually this is a servant's reply meaning 'I'm coming' or 'In a moment'. Here Tony means 'I'm coming to see what you mean' or 'Explain yourself further'

Act 3 Scene 1

This Act consists of one scene, where Kate indicates her interest in Marlow. Mr Hardcastle wonders how she takes to him; when they compare notes he thinks that Marlow is impudent and familiar, but she had found him timid and sullen. But they decide not to reject him if he can alter the impressions he has created on his first appearance – Kate thinks there may be good qualities in him, though her father is convinced of his impudence. They leave the stage, and Tony enters with Constance's jewels in a casket which he has secretly taken from his mother's bureau, to which he has a key. He gives them to Hastings, who tells him Constance is trying to get them from Mrs Hardcastle. Tony advises Hastings to clear off, as Mrs Hardcastle and Constance are coming. Constance argues that she wants to show the jewels as relics for a day, but Mrs Hardcastle – urged on privately by Tony – informs her that they are lost. Mrs Hardcastle then offers to lend her own garnets to Constance instead of the 'missing' jewels, and goes off to get them. Meanwhile Tony urges Constance to take the garnets, saying that he's stolen her jewels from his mother's bureau for her. He tells her to vanish, just as his mother returns, greatly upset now that she has found Constance's jewels aren't in her bureau. Tony mocks her until she pursues him from the stage.

Kate enters with her maid; she now realises that Tony has been responsible for Marlow and Hastings thinking the house is an inn. The maid tells her that Marlow thinks she is the barmaid; he has just seen her in her household dress and doesn't realise she is Kate Hardcastle, because he never looked up when he talked to her earlier, and her face was hidden in her bonnet. The maid leaves, telling her Marlow is coming. Kate disguises her voice when he arrives and he indulges in a flirtation with her. He has seized her in an embrace only to be interrupted by the arrival of Hardcastle, at which he rushes off, while Hardcastle expresses his astonishment to Kate, accusing her of deceiving him. She says she will convince him Marlow is modest. Hardcastle, however, won't be convinced at all, and tells her he is thinking of turning him out of the house: but then he accedes to Kate's request to give her an hour more to convince him that Marlow is the man she thinks he is.

NOTES AND GLOSSARY:

piece of brass: an impertinent, brazen person

mauvaise honte: *(French)* bashfulness, foolish shamefacedness

Bully Dawson: a well-known ruffian who lived in Whitefriars (a locality in London frequented by criminals) at the time of the play

the rest . . . furniture: the rest of his accomplishments and abilities

bobs: earrings or pendants

my genus: this may be a corruption of 'genius' or 'Jesus'

amused: bemused, deceived her

bear your charges: pay your expenses

fibs: lies

rule of thumb: rough and ready methods

bounce of a cracker: I don't care; it is like 'a snap of the finger'

Morrice! Prance!: move off quickly. Morrice is connected with Morris-dance

my lady Killdaylight and Mrs Cramp: the first name is obviously a joke; the second means crooked or hump-backed

paste: artificial material, giving the appearance of diamonds

marcasites: iron pyrites in crystallized form: they can be polished and then resemble gold or silver

rose-cut and table-cut things: rose-cut stones have a round, smooth face, made-up of small facets; table-cut stones have a flat facet, surrounded by smaller ones

court . . . puppet-show: King Soloman's court was renowned for its wealth. This was probably simulated in puppet shows by a lot of vulgar decoration

Show them as relics: Constance is being bitter. Relics in the Christian tradition are objects, pieces of the body, clothing or articles of personal use which remain as memorials of a holy person or saint. They are very precious and tend to be shown on rare occasions

garnets:	semi-precious stones, unfashionable at this period, considered more suitable for older women than girls
your spark:	your flame, lover, boy-friend
Catharine-wheel:	a rotating firework, called after St Catharine of Alexandria, martyred on a spiked wheel in 307AD
Cherry:	Cherry was the landlord's daughter in *The Beaux Stratagem* (1707), a sparkling comedy by George Farquhar (1677–1707) which has often been revived with great success

The Lion . . . the Angel . . . the Lamb: inn rooms were named rather than numbered at this period

outrageous:	clamorous
tablets:	material for writing on, usually a set or pair hinged or fastened together
malicious:	mischievous
nectar:	in classical mythology, the drink of the Gods; any delicious drink, or the honey produced by plants, collected by bees
French wines:	there was a high tax on French wine, and so smuggling flourished
mark of mouth:	a horse's age can be told by an examination of its teeth
obstropalous:	a word made-up to resemble a dialect form; obstreperous, noisy
dash'd:	abashed
rallied:	teased
the Ladies' Club:	a reference to a coterie of women in Albemarle Street, London, to which men were admitted
Rattle:	a chatterer, gossip-monger
Biddy Buckskin:	originally a reference to a Miss Rachael Lloyd, a member of the coterie, but 'Rachael Buckskin' was altered to 'Biddy Buckskin' after the first performance
time they all have:	she implies they can't have much time for their husbands or families after spending their time gossiping in the club
nicked Seven:	to nick seven was to bet on throwing a six and a one. Ames ace (ambs-ace, both aces) was the lowest possible score, two ones. Throwing it three times after hazarding money on a seven meant bad luck, because each time he had thrown the one ace needed, and had to throw a six to win

Act 4 Scene 1

This is another single scene act. In it Hastings learns from Constance that Sir Charles Marlow is expected, and he decides that they must leave quickly, as Sir Charles knows him. He tells her that he has sent the jewels to Marlow and goes off to prepare for their elopement. Constance leaves in order to pretend to her aunt that she has a passion for Tony. Marlow comes in, baffled by Hastings having sent him the casket to keep. He has instructed his servant to give it to the landlady, so the jewels are back in Mrs Hardcastle's possession. Marlow's interest in the supposed barmaid continues; she 'runs through his head most strangely'. He tells Hastings of how he is attracted by her when he returns and also lets him know that he's given the casket to the landlady. Hastings accepts the fact that his and Constance's hopes of a fortune have vanished and leaves.

Hardcastle comes in, infuriated by the fact that Marlow's servants have been drinking. Marlow sends for one of them, and tells him to inform the landlord that he had orders from Marlow to drink freely. Hardcastle orders Marlow to leave the house, and Marlow in a rage demands his bill. But as Hardcastle storms off, telling Marlow he will make his father aware of his son's behaviour, it begins to dawn on Marlow that the house may not be an inn. Kate enters, and realises that he is beginning to discover his mistake, but decides it is too soon to undeceive him; she tells him she is no barmaid, just a poor relation. And he regrets that he must leave; he will do so with reluctance. An honourable solution isn't possible, and he would never seduce her because she trusts his honour. He has been moved by her pretending to cry; then, by her saying that she regrets she has no money since this puts her at a distance 'from one, that if I had a thousand pounds I would give it all to'. Marlow decides he must make the effort to leave her; he is bound to carry out his father's wishes, and so he says farewell to her. After he has gone and before she leaves she decides she will undeceive her father, that she will not let Marlow go.

Tony and Constance come in, and decide to seem fond of each other, in case Mrs Hardcastle suspects Constance is planning to run away. Mrs Hardcastle enters, now thinking that the jewels were lost through a mistake of the servants. She decides Tony and Constance will be married next day, but then Diggory brings in a letter for Tony. This is from Hastings. Constance tries to draw Mrs Hardcastle's attention from Tony's difficulty in reading the letter; then she pretends to read it to Tony herself. But she excites Tony's curiosity too much by what she invents. She crumples up the letter, telling him it is of no consequence; but he then gives it to his mother who finds it is from Hastings, saying he is waiting with a postchaise and horses at the bottom of the garden but needs a fresh pair of horses from Tony. He adds that there is a need for speed in case Mrs Hardcastle suspects them.

Mrs Hardcastle is furious, and decides to use the fresh horses to take Constance at once to her Aunt Pedigree, who will keep her secure. She orders Tony to accompany them on his horse. When she goes off Tony and Constance indulge in recriminations, and Hastings comes in, enraged with Tony for having shown the letter and thus betrayed their plans of running away. Marlow arrives, furious now that he has discovered Tony's trick in telling them that the house was an inn. Both young men attack Tony, but then Marlow turns on Hastings for not undeceiving him. There comes a message that Constance is to leave. Marlow and Hastings continue to argue, the servant enters again with Constance's cloak, then her fan, muff and gloves, and the news that Mrs Hardcastle is impatient to be off. Constance pacifies the friends, and asks Hastings to be constant for the three years it will take for her to be free to marry him. After she has left, Marlow turns on Tony, but Tony has had an idea, and tells Marlow and Hastings to meet him in two hours' time at the bottom of the garden.

NOTES AND GLOSSARY:

post-coach: a coach which would use post-horses hired to travellers by those who had the charge of posting establishments at intervals on the post-roads. The two young men came in a post-chaise, we are told earlier; this is presumably the same vehicle which Hastings intends to use to take Constance to France

liberty . . . Fleet Street: a reference to the taverns in Fleet Street, London

soused: completely immersed

a puddle in a storm: this idiom means the same as 'a storm in a teacup'

The Rake's Progress: a famous set of prints (published in 1753) by the artist William Hogarth (1697–1764). These show the progressive ruin of a young man given to the pursuit of pleasure

coxcomb: conceited person, a fop

in caricatura: many caricatures of well known people were available in the print shops

the Dullissimo Maccaroni: *(Italian)* the most stupid maccaroni, a reference to the Macaronis, young dandies who dressed in foreign styles. They were supposed to enjoy eating Italian macaroni. In the 1770s they wore red-heeled shoes, small cocked hats, and close cut jackets, waistcoats and breeches, and affected a large knot of artificial hair; they carried long tasselled walking sticks

sensibly:	he means his deeper feelings are involved
I stoop'd to conquer:	a line in *The Hind and the Panther* (1685) by the poet, playwright and essayist John Dryden (1631–1700) is said to have suggested the title of the play to Goldsmith: 'But kneels to conquer and but stoops to rise'
Whistle-jacket:	a racehorse famous for its running at York and Newmarket in 1754; it was owned by Lord Rockingham.
in a pound:	an enclosure where straying cattle were placed; their owners could redeem them on paying a fine
haspicholls:	a malapropism (so called after Mrs Malaprop, a character in *The Rivals* (1775) a comedy by Richard Brinsley Sheridan. She mis-applied long words, getting their meanings wrong) for harpsichords; a harpsichord was an early form of piano
parcel of bobbins:	wooden bobbins used in making lace: the thread is held by them, and a skilled lace-maker moves them to and fro very quickly
incontinently:	immediately
mun:	must
cramp:	cramped
an izzard:	the letter 'z'
the feeder:	a man who fattened up cattle for slaughter; here possibly someone looking after fighting cocks
Shake-bag:	a large fighting cock
odd battle . . . long fighting:	betting terms
so nice:	over-clever, over-subtle
old Bedlam:	Bedlam, the hospital of St Mary of Bethlehem, the lunatic asylum in St George's Fields, London. Tony means there will soon be as much noise and quarrelling as if the inhabitants of a lunatic asylum had broken out
baskets:	single sticks, so called from their wicker handguards

Act 5 Scene 1

Hastings learns from a servant that Mrs Hardcastle has taken Constance off in a post-coach, with Tony accompanying them on horseback. He also hears that Sir Charles Marlow has arrived and that he and Mr Hardcastle are laughing about Marlow's mistaking the house for an inn. He goes off to keep his appointment with Tony though he thinks it has no point, since Tony and the coach will be, as the servant has said, thirty miles away.

Sir Charles Marlow and Mr Hardcastle enter, discussing the marriage of Marlow and Kate. Sir Charles questions Marlow's liking for her. Marlow enters, apologises to Hardcastle, but says he has never given Miss Hardcastle – he is very formal – any mark of attachment. He tells his father that he saw the lady without emotion and parted without reluctance. He leaves the scene, having astonished both fathers. Kate then enters, and in answer to questioning says that Marlow and she have had more than one interview that he has made professions of love to her. Finally she persuades her father and Sir Charles to hide behind a screen in about half an hour's time and says they will hear him declare his passion to her.

NOTES AND GLOSSARY:

behind that screen: concealment behind a screen is a device frequently used in comedy – the most notable example probably occuring in Sheridan's *The School for Scandal* (1777)

Act 5 Scene 2

Hastings is surprised to find Tony keeping their appointment. It is dark, and he tells Hastings – after some complaining and some comic descriptions of the twenty-five mile roundabout journey – that he has finally lodged the coach in the horse-pond at the bottom of the garden. He says his mother, who thinks she is forty miles from home, is terrified, and he advises Hastings to take Constance off if his horses are ready, since none of theirs, being exhausted, will be able to follow them. When Hastings thanks him he rebukes him for his earlier abuse, but, seeing his mother coming – she has waded through the pond – tells Hastings to vanish.

When Mrs Hardcastle arrives Tony teases her, telling her they are on Crackskull Common, a notoriously dangerous place for highwaymen, but then she sees a man approaching. Tony realises that it is his stepfather, but, telling his mother it is a highwayman, he persuades her to hide in a thicket, saying he will cough and cry 'hem' if there is danger. He then conducts a conversation with Mr Hardcastle, while trying to keep his mother hidden in the thicket by coughing and crying out 'hem'. Mr Hardcastle hears another voice, but Tony pretends that he is talking to himself about the forty mile journey he says he's taken to bring his mother and Constance to Aunt Pedigree's. Mr Hardcastle insists on finding out who is there, but his wife rushes out, and, thinking him a highwayman, begs for mercy. Mr Hardcastle then tells her where she really is, and she pursues Tony in a fine fury.

After Mr Hardcastle has followed Tony and his wife, Hastings and Constance Neville arrive. He urges her to fly with him, but she decides to stay and not to lose her fortune. She decides to appeal to Mr Hardcastle and, reluctantly, Hastings agrees they should stay.

NOTES AND GLOSSARY:

smoked:	the horses have steamed as a result of their hard work
rabbit me:	confound me; from rabattre *(French)* to beat down
varment:	corruption of 'vermin'
mon:	man
by jingo:	an exclamation of surprise, originally a piece of conjurer's gibberish
circumbendibus:	a roundabout way; a piece of pseudo-Latin, *circum (Latin)* meaning around
the cattle:	the horses
whip off:	rush off
kiss the hangman:	condemned criminals often kissed the hangman as a sign of forgiveness
without knowing one inch of the way:	it was dark, and earlier in the play Mrs Hardcastle has said not a creature but themselves did not take a trip to town now and then. So her being lost is not improbable
Father-in-law:	old fashioned term for stepfather
pistoils:	pistols

Act 5 Scene 3

This scene opens with Sir Charles Marlow talking to Kate. He tells her that he is in an awkward situation. If she is right his son is a liar; if what Marlow says is true he will lose Kate whom he wishes to be his daughter-in-law. She says he and her father will hear a declaration from Marlow, sees him coming and urges Sir Charles to go off and get her father so they can both hide themselves behind the screen. Marlow tells Kate that he is torn between pride and passion. She replies that though she is of as good family as the girl he came down to visit, and though her education is not inferior, money matters. He should go, since all his aims are to find a fortune.

At this stage Sir Charles and Mr Hardcastle sit behind the screen and hear Marlow praising Kate's beauty and her innocence and virtue. He tells her that he has determined to stay, that his father will approve of her. She says that she will not detain him; she will not take advantage of his transient passion; she will not acquire her happiness by lessening his. He continues to say that he will stay; she replies she will not entertain a connection where she must seem mercenary and he imprudent. Finally Sir Charles and Mr Hardcastle interrupt him and accuse him of having one story for them and one for Kate. Suddenly he realises Kate is Mr Hardcastle's daughter. She teases him, reminding him of his earlier appearance – as the faltering shy gentleman, and then as the loud self-confident friend of Mrs Mantrap and Miss Biddy Buckskin. When yet again he says he must be gone, Mr Hardcastle tells him it was all a mistake and Kate will forgive him.

Kate continues to tease Marlow at the back of the stage, when Mrs Hardcastle and Tony enter. Mrs Hardcastle says that Hastings and Constance have eloped. Sir Charles says Hastings is a good choice but Mrs Hardcastle argues that Constance's fortune remains in the Hardcastle family. She reminds her husband that if Tony when he is of age (when he is twenty-one)refuses to marry his cousin her fortune is at her own disposal, to which Mr Hardcastle replies that Constance has not waited for Tony's refusal, and he is not yet of age. At this point Hastings and Constance return. He reminds Mr Hardcastle that he had first paid his addresses to her with her father's consent; Constance's appeal to Mr Hardcastle is for more generous treatment than she has received from his wife. Hardcastle reveals that Tony *is* of age, that his mother had kept this secret. Tony's first act is to refuse Constance, so that she can marry whom she pleases. Hastings persuades Kate to accept Marlow, and Hardcastle rounds off the play by inviting everyone to supper with the promise of a party for the poor of the parish next day. The mistakes of a night shall be crowned, he says, with a merry morning.

NOTES AND GLOSSARY:

the whining end . . . novel: Mrs Hardcastle is describing novels which distinguish between the fates of 'good' and 'bad' characters

the mistakes of a night: this was the play's secondary title

Part 3

Commentary

The plot

Goldsmith used a reputed experience he had as a schoolboy in Ireland as the basis of his plot. He had lost his way, asked for an inn, and been directed by a practical joker to the local squire's house. He behaved in a lordly way there, but when he called for his bill in the morning discovered that the man he had taken for an innkeeper was a friend of his father's from their undergraduate days. To the situation created by his own experience of a practical joke Goldsmith added some typical ingredients of comedy: two pairs of lovers, the apparent battle between the young and the old, and characters of considerable individuality: Tony Lumpkin, a great piece of comic invention, Mr and Mrs Hardcastle, and Marlow.

This plot allowed Goldsmith variety. The sub-title *The Mistakes of a Night* conveys this, for the possibilities of mistakes are explored to the full, and they follow in quick succession. The humour of the play depends, in part, upon the audience knowing more of the truth than the characters themselves. It is worth studying how Goldsmith gives us the necessary information about what is happening, for he does this with great skill, unobtrusively and economically. Take, for instance, the first act, which has to inform us quickly about the characters. We see that Mr and Mrs Hardcastle are different in age and temperament, that they live in a rambling old house that looks like an inn (thus we are prepared for the practical joke), that they don't often have company (which prepares us for the special preparations they make for the guests).

We learn that Tony is Mr Hardcastle's step-son, that his stepfather dislikes his habit of practical joking, and we see a little of his rumbustious nature. We see Kate as different, an obedient girl who explains why she is wearing a housewife's dress – a fact that is significant in the plot later when Marlow mistakes her for a servant. We realise she is in a flutter over her father's plan to marry her to Marlow, who is eligible and handsome, but reserved and shy. We learn that Marlow is a friend of Hastings, who is Constance Neville's admirer, she being an orphan whose guardian is Mrs Hardcastle. Mrs Hardcastle wants to marry Constance to Tony. Constance has a fortune in jewels and pretends to care for Tony who doesn't want to marry her; but she really is in love with Hastings. Here, then, are the ingredients all clearly told to us. What will Goldsmith make of them?

The complications begin virtually at once, for Constance shows us that Tony is more amicable than he might seem. We hear, too, that Marlow is less modest than he might seem, and we realise Mrs Hardcastle doesn't know that Constance is not in love with Tony. The characters leave the stage to pursue actions which contribute to the play's movement. All of this is very rapidly achieved; we have realised things in general are not at all what they seem, and our interest is captured. It is to be retained throughout the play, as yet more complications crowd in.

The third act, the centre of the plot, clearly shows Goldsmith's ability to construct, and to convey suspense. Here, for instance, we have an opening where Hardcastle and Kate discuss Marlow, each having formed a different idea about him. We can understand why, for we have seen his different behaviours with the supposed innkeeper and with Kate, the young lady of social standing. This leaves Kate, her father – and ourselves – wondering what kind of man Marlow really is.

We switch to the almost farcical business with the jewels where Tony wilfully misunderstands his mother, hugely enjoying the irony of the situation. Next we are back to the problem of Marlow, the scene between the maid and Kate preparing us for the flirtation which ensues. We realise how Kate is mocking him. When Hardcastle enters we see that he is amazed by her descriptions of Marlow; she persuades her father to let her prove that Marlow is really a modest man. Though he agrees, when he imposes the time limit of an hour, a note of urgency is imparted to the action, and this urgency is immediately reinforced in the beginning of the next act when we hear Sir Charles Marlow is about to arrive. Hastings and Constance have to achieve their plan, they must get away before he comes, because he knows Hastings; so their need for quick action is added to Kate's. There is the complication of Marlow's having sent Constance's jewels to Mrs Hardcastle – and then he discovers that he is not in an Inn, and he wants to leave quickly.

Everything speeds up. In a moment the elopement plot is betrayed – after the suspense of Constance's reading the letter. And this suspense matches the speed. For instance, the three entries of the servant to tell Constance to get ready to leave at once add to the tension, and Mrs Hardcastle's shouting at her from within gives extra urgency to the quarrel between Marlow and Hastings which Constance wants to stop.

There is much more to enjoy. The problem of the true nature of Marlow perplexes his father and Hardcastle. We are told about the adventures of the coach, so that we see the absurdity of Mrs Hardcastle's taking her husband for a highwayman. And we have the final occasion when Marlow is made a fool of, when Goldsmith uses the screen to conceal the two fathers and let them overhear Marlow's declaration to Kate. We have a classic exposure too, at the last moment, when Hardcastle reveals Tony's true age and his right to his fortune, and Mrs Hardcastle's plans are thus frustrated. Both sets of lovers are united, while Tony, no doubt, is now free to pursue his Bet Bouncer.

The characters

The major characters

Mr Hardcastle loves everything old; he thinks that the times in which he lives are infected by fashion. He can be very boring; he repeats his views, as we are told by his wife very early in the first scene. And we hear from the servants in Act II, Scene I that he repeats his stories as well, and he bores the young men (also in Act II Scene I) with his reminiscences of the war. But he is not stupid; he realises his step-son Tony's true nature, and he also knows that his wife has spoiled him. But although he thinks his daughter Kate has almost been influenced by the fashions of the time he is fond of her, and he tells her he will not inflict a husband on her whom she doesn't like; he will not control her choice. His relationship with her is obviously an easy and pleasant one.

Hardcastle is courteous and hospitable to his guests. Though he is amazed by their arrogance he keeps his annoyance to himself, surprised that Marlow does not live up to his reputation for modesty, surprised, too, by both of them ordering him around in his own house, and by their impudent comments on the menu for dinner. He discusses Marlow freely with Kate; their views are very different. He tells her how

> He spoke to me as if he knew me all his life before. Asked twenty questions, and never waited for an answer. Interrupted my best remarks with some silly pun, and when I was in my best story of the Duke of Marlborough and Prince Eugene, he asked if I had not a good hand at making punch. Yes, Kate, he ask'd your father if he was a maker of punch.

However, he has not got a completely closed mind, for he tells her if 'young Mr Brazen can find the art of reconciling contradictions' he may please them both. Though Hardcastle is angry when he finds Kate struggling with Marlow (in Act III, Scene I) and tells her he is thinking of turning Marlow out of the house that very hour, he is prepared to give her time to prove Marlow is modest. But the provocation he receives (in Act IV Scene I) is just too much for him. Marlow's frank admission that he ordered his servants to drink freely stirs him into ordering Marlow to leave the house immediately; he tells him how different he is from his father's account of him.

By the time Sir Charles Marlow arrives, Hardcastle has learned from Kate about Marlow's mistaking the house for an inn, and Hardcastle can enjoy the joke; and share it with Sir Charles. He is ready to accept the young man as a son-in-law, since Kate has as good as told him she and Marlow like each other. He finds Marlow's denial of having given Kate 'the slightest mark' of his attachment baffling; he has complete faith in Kate, and does not object to her plan of showing him and Sir Charles how Marlow *does* care for her.

His blunt speech to his wife when she thinks him a highwayman is matched by his recognising how truly Tony has put the situation when he blames his mother for spoiling him. And after he and Sir Charles have overheard from behind the screen Marlow's talk with Kate he realises fairly quickly (in Act V, Scene III) how Marlow's behaviour has arisen through his mistake, and tells him Kate will forgive him. His amiability extends to Constance. He takes a moral view of Mrs Hardcastle's plot to keep Tony's true age secret, in which he has previously concurred, and, now that she is turning it not to Tony's improvement but to a wrong use, he exposes it. He rounds off the play with a general air of merriment and benevolence.

Mr Hardcastle is, thus, grumbling and irascible, opinionatedly boring, but generally kindly; and, in his way, he is a classic father of comedy, deceived but forgiving.

Mrs Hardcastle is very unlike her husband. She begins the play by grousing about his not taking her anywhere. She spoils Tony yet she conceals his age, and she worries unnecessarily about his health. She wants him to marry Constance Neville, being unwilling to let Constance's fortune in jewels go out of the family. She doesn't allow Constance to wear the jewellery (I.I). She is vain enough to accept Hasting's flattering remarks about her hair, and is obvious in her attempted match-making between Tony and Constance (II.I). She complains that she never sees Tony when he is cheerful. At his prompting she has told Constance that the jewels are missing, but when she discovers that the jewels actually have been taken from her bureau (by Tony, though she doesn't realise this) and is mocked by Tony, who pretends that she is pretending they are lost, she chases him in a passion.

When the jewels are deposited with her by Marlow (who hasn't realised what is in the casket Hastings sent him to keep, and still doesn't realise Mrs Hardcastle isn't the landlady of an inn) she thinks it has been a mistake of the servants, and renews her efforts to effect a marriage between Tony and Constance, and says Constance shall have the jewels and the pair be married the next day (IV.I).

She is naturally infuriated when she discovers that Hastings and Constance have planned to elope, with Tony helping them by providing a pair of fresh horses, and she is prompt to take Constance off to her Aunt Pedigree.

Her genuine concern for Tony emerges (in Act V, Scene II) when she thinks Mr Hardcastle is a highwayman; again she pursues him in her rage once she discovers how she's been deceived. When she thinks that Hastings and Constance have succeeded in eloping, she intends to keep Constance's jewels – and does not like the couple returning so soon. Her last speech in the midst of the general good will is to proclaim Tony undutiful for refusing Constance's hand.

Mrs Hardcastle is not, then, an entirely likeable character; vain, gullible, unkind; quite ready to turn on Tony, whom she earlier spoils, by now calling him a fool, a booby, a monster and a blockhead. Her response to Constance's appeal to Mr Hardcastle for fair play is contemptuous: 'this is all but the whining end of a modern novel'. She is a grouser, a nagger – as Tony describes her, 'dinging it, dinging it into one so'. (She resembles Mrs Primrose, the vicar's wife in Goldsmith's novel *The Vicar of Wakefield* – who was probably founded on Goldsmith's own mother, who seems to have been a match-maker who encouraged her daughters into affectation and extravagance).

Tony Lumpkin is the character who develops most in the play. We first see him as the spoiled son of his mother, an ungracious, un-responsive bumpkin, determined to get to his friends in the alehouse (Act I, Scene I). There, however, he is a popular figure, singing a song, standing drinks, and looking forward to his coming of age, when he will get an income of fifteen hundred pounds a year (then a large sum). He dislikes his stepfather, and seizes the opportunity to play a trick on him and on the smart young men who arrive at the Inn by directing them to Mr Hardcastle's house and telling them it is an inn. He is intelligent enough to tell them that the landlord would like to be thought a gentleman and is likely to give them his company, to treat them as equals. This ensures that the joke is likely to work in its initial stages, since the young men will simply think Hardcastle is an eccentric kind of innkeeper.

Tony, however, seems to shed his dislike of his stepfather during the play; his joke against him arises out of his instinctive sense of fun, his liking to play jokes on people. His attitude to his mother is different. He does not want to be married off to Constance; he obviously fancies Bet Bouncer, who never appears in the play; and so he aids Constance and Hastings, taking their part and deceiving his mother. He is for fair play; his mother's keeping back his inheritance seems unreasonable (indeed we learn in the last scene that it has been dishonest), and so he secretly takes his money from his mother's bureau for spending at the alehouse with a clear conscience: 'An honest man may rob himself of his own at any time'. He is not afraid of his mother and says 'I don't value her resentment the bounce of a cracker' (Act III).

He is clever in suggesting to her that she should pretend Constance's jewels are missing, and he supports her when she tells Constance this. The audience knows he's stolen them and given them to Hastings and so his speech 'That I can bear witness to they are missing, and not to be found, I'll take my oath on 't' (III.I) has a nice irony about it. But when his mother discovers that the jewels have really disappeared his treatment of her distress shows his cleverness even more. By pretending to be a blockhead, by pretending his mother is pretending the jewels have gone, he creates a situation of some absurdity, and his repetition of 'I can bear witness to that', the phrase he used earlier when pretending to Constance that the jewels were 'missing', intensifies the ironic complexity of this highly comic scene.

Tony enjoys the situations he creates. When he has brought his mother back to the pond, he describes what he has done in riddling terms to Hastings; he has brought the coach round all the ponds and sloughs within five miles of the house. And when his mother struggles up from the pond he tells her the discomfort is her own fault for 'running away by night, without knowing one inch of the way'. Then he heightens her fears by pretending he sees highwaymen, next explains them away by saying they are trees or cows, only to have to use his invention more particularly when his stepfather approaches.

There is a strength of purpose in Tony, a capacity for more than clowning. When his plans go wrong he is not downhearted. After Mrs Hardcastle has got the jewels back he still is ready to help Constance and Hastings, even to the extent of pretending to be enamoured of Constance (IV.I). Once Constance has been too clever in pretending to read Hasting's letter to Tony, and has failed to prevent Mrs Hardcastle from knowing what is in it, Tony accepts the situation as it is. Constance says 'So now I'm completely ruined', to which he replies, 'Ay, that's a sure thing'. He tells her she was at fault, and when Hastings and Marlow both abuse him in turn he remarks of each 'Here's another'. He resents their calling him 'a mere boy, an idiot whose ignorance and age are a protection' and 'a poor contemptible booby, that would but disgrace correction', and is ready to fight the two clever young men, one after the other. But when they are in despair, it is he who contrives the idea which will eventually – through his bringing the coach back to the pond – resolve the situation for Constance and Hastings.

Tony, then, despite his lack of polish, and his ignorance of fashionable ways, displays an impressive quickwitted ability to manage an intrigue; he is generous and exuberant, and he appeals to an audience by his lively outspokenness. Country wit and country ways are at work here, and though Tony may lack polish Goldsmith gives him, very skilfully, a complex character.

Kate Hardcastle is an inventive, lively girl; at first she seems demure and dutiful, rather the opposite of Tony. She accepts her father's suggestion of Marlow as a suitor with natural curiosity; she is modest as she weighs up Marlow's pros and cons – 'But I vow I'm disposing of the husband before I have secured the lover'.

Her formal meeting with the bashful Marlow (II.I) is followed by her weighing him up. 'If I could teach him a little confidence, it would be doing somebody I know of a piece of service'. And then she decides, once she hears Marlow has thought her – in her ordinary dress – to be a barmaid, to act the part. She enjoys it, so much so that she persuades her father not to turn him out of the house at least for an hour. She begins to like Marlow, even to admire him, once he discovers his mistake in taking the Hardcastles' house for an Inn. When he makes her his speech of farewell she decides very firmly 'He shall not go, if I have power or art to detain him'.

She is determined, and persuasive, convincing her father and Sir Charles that they should hide themselves behind the screen, to allow her to prove Marlow's true nature to them. And her delight in him emerges in fond teasing once he has realised who she really is.

Constance Neville, Kate's cousin, has already decided whom she wants to marry. She is in love with Hastings, her father had approved of him before he died, but Mrs Hardcastle, who is her guardian and has the sole management of Constance's fortune, wishes her to marry her son Tony Lumpkin as she does not want the fortune to go out of the family. Constance lets her think that she is in love with Tony; she wants her aunt to let her wear the jewels, and she tells Hastings 'The instant they are put into my possession you shall find me ready to make them and myself yours' (II.I). She is disturbed, not unnaturally, when Mrs Hardcastle says they are mislaid: but when she hears Tony has stolen them and given them to Hastings, she is quick to say to Hastings that she hopes they are safe (IV.I). However, once the jewels have been regained by Mrs Hardcastle, her fear is only that her aunt may suspect she is about to elope with Hastings.

She acts her part of pretending to love Tony and is successful with Mrs Hardcastle until she makes her fatal mistake in inventing false contents for Hasting's letter to Tony, on whom she, like Hastings and

Marlow, turns when the plot is exposed. She pacifies Hastings and Marlow who are quarrelling and then emphasises the need for constancy (there is a subdued form of punning on Constance and constancy here) for three years.

Once she is brought back to the garden and can now elope with Hastings her common-sense asserts itself: 'Prudence once more comes to my relief, and I will obey its dictates. In the moment of passion, fortune may be despised, but it ever produces a lasting repentance' (V.II). She decides to appeal to Mr Hardcastle's sense of compassion and justice, his capacity to influence: and she is wise in this. When she and Hastings return she shows how her acting has been different from Kate's. Kate stooped to conquer her lover. But since her father's death, Constance says, she has been obliged 'to stoop to dissimulation to avoid oppression' – in other words, to pretend to love Tony, though her love for Hastings had been approved by her father, adding that in an hour of levity she was ready even to give up her fortune to secure her choice. Now, however, she hopes that Mr Hardcastle's tenderness will give her what his wife has not.

She is thus sensible and determined, but the duplicity in which she and Hastings were engaged incurred the risks of discovery. They did not tell Marlow Mr Hardcastle was not an innkeeper; their first attempt at escape depended upon Tony's help with fresh horses; their second was made possible by his stratagem of bringing the coach round in a circle. Her attitude is not entirely a romantic one; she has her feet firmly on the ground – for most of the time.

Marlow is an unusual character, shy and unsure of himself in approaching ladies, over-confident as a would-be conqueror of barmaids. He seems contradictory: ready to obey his father's arrangements for his marriage, yet finding Miss Kate Hardcastle over-prim when he first meets her. When he thinks the supposed barmaid is a poor relation, he seems at first determined to avoid becoming entangled with her. These differing attitudes are part and parcel of eighteenth century and earlier attitudes to marriage: it was generally unromantic, generally arranged by parents and based upon the need to cement alliances of families or fortunes. But Marlow's sense of pride gives way to his passionate regard for the poor relative, whose beauty, grace, refined simplicity, courageous innocence and conscious virtue he praises; he is sure his father will approve of her.

By all that's good, I can have no happiness but what's in your power to grant me. Nor shall I ever feel repentance, but in not having seen your merits before . . . I will make my respectful assiduities a tone for the levity of my past conduct.

He has developed, and become worthy of Kate who has discerned his potential capacity to become a genuine lover.

Marlow is an unusual hero in the sense that he is to a certain extent a 'gull' in the comedy – he is the object of a joke. Like Mr Hardcastle, he is made a fool of through Tony's describing the Hardcastles' house as an inn, but, more significantly, he is also made a fool of by Kate's stooping to the role of barmaid. These two deceptions make his character clear. He has been described as modest, but Mr Hardcastle finds him impudent when he cuts short the supposed innkeeper's anecdotes. (In this comedy of errors Marlow himself thinks the landlord is a very impudent fellow). Where his shyness and modesty appear is in the first interview with Kate – when he gazes on the ground, awkwardly addressing the Miss Hardcastle he has come to see. This scene has to be well staged, so that he does not notice her closely. Her dress must be very different when he sees her as the barmaid – when, as we are told, she also adopts a different voice.

We see Marlow's extremes of behaviour through Mr Hardcastle's and Kate's eyes alternatively; once she realises the ironic situation about the young men mistaking the house for an inn she has the chance to tease Marlow, to try him out and discover that the extremes of his character add up to one personality capable of honour and affection. And the smart young man of the city is conquered by the country girl, who might not have seemed a match for him at the beginning of the play. How far his unusual nature was founded upon aspects of Goldsmith's own character we can't tell, but the parallels are there – Goldsmith was duped by a joker when he was misdirected to the house of one of his father's friends as if to an inn; he himself experienced the pangs of feeling himself to be a fool; he was sensitive about his appearance; he liked to dress well, as Marlow does; and his poverty had probably kept him from the company of women of his own social status for a considerable part of his life.

George Hastings is a less interesting character. He is in love with Constance, uninterested in her fortune. He wants her to elope to France with him, and when she tells him that he and Marlow are in the Hardcastles' house he persuades her not to tell Marlow of the mistake because he would leave the house instantly and thus ruin their plan. He has smooth manners. For instance, he tries to encourage Marlow when he meets Kate, he flatters Mrs Hardcastle, and he is quick to tell Tony he'll take Constance off if Tony will help him. He is also disturbed when he hears that Tony has stolen the jewels because he thinks if Constance persuades Mrs Hardcastle to give them to her 'it will be the most delicate way at least of obtaining them' (Act III, Scene I).

Hastings isn't very efficient, for when he does get the jewels from
Tony he sends them to Marlow to keep (Marlow is surprised at this:
'I wonder what Hastings could mean by sending me so valuable a thing
as a casket to keep for him . . .'); and because he and Constance have
left Marlow ignorant about the Inn actually being the Hardcastles'
house he can't explain to Marlow how his leaving the casket with the
landlady has ruined their hopes of taking Constance's fortune with
them. His equanimity about this – a sign of his unmercenary attitude
to Constance, which contrasts with Marlow's approach to marriage
before he falls in love with Kate – is replaced by rage when he hears
Mrs Hardcastle has read his letter to Tony and thus decided to take
Constance away: 'My heart. How can I support this? To be so near
happiness, and such happiness? Hastings has an innate dignity; he
accepts Tony's rebuke once he hears Constance is back. He then urges
her to run off with him, but finally gives in to her arguments and
agrees to face Mr Hardcastle, making a direct and dignified speech of
apology for his behaviour to him.

The minor characters

The Landlord is a bluff character, but he takes a hint quickly from Tony;
having first queried what he intends:

'Sure, you ben't sending them to your father's as an inn, be you?'
(I.II)

he plays up to him well; he enjoys Tony's character and calls him
'a sweet, pleasant – damn'd mischievous son of a whore'.

Diggory and **Roger** are servants whom Mr Hardcastle has brought from
the barn and the plough – in other words they have been farm
workers, and find it difficult to act as efficient servants.

The Maid has a small role, but a significant one. She has to make clear
to the audience that Kate knows, by Act III, Scene I, that Tony has
misdirected the young men about the house being an inn, that
Marlow hasn't recognised Kate in her changed dress and thinks she is a
barmaid. She also asks Kate what she will gain by pretending to be a
barmaid, and asks whether she can act the part and disguise her voice.

Sir Charles Marlow is an old friend of Mr Hardcastle. He is not worried
that Kate hasn't a large dowry; he wants to be sure the young couple
like each other. But he can't believe his son capable of lying about his
behaviour to Miss Hardcastle, even though Kate herself describes his

behaviour to her. However, he agrees to her suggestion and when he hears (from behind the screen) Marlow making his declaration to her he can stand it no longer, and taxes his son with deceiving him. However, the mistake is cleared up, and Sir George aids Hastings's cause by praising him before he returns with Constance to seek agreement about their marriage. Sir Charles is an amiable character, helpful and enthusiastic, as his last brief speech shows clearly: 'O brave Squire', he cries, praising Tony's refusal of Constance.

Language and style

Goldsmith delineates his characters in a subtle way: they have their own mannerisms, their own ways of speech. Notice, for instance, how in Act I, Scene I Hardcastle prefaces many of his remarks with 'Ay'. Marlow, when speaking to Kate in his respectable vein, begins most of his replies with 'Yes, madam'. And Tony's use of 'Ecod' and other oaths is characteristic of him.

Goldsmith makes his characters' speeches link together through repetition. For instance,

HASTINGS: Well, but where have you left the ladies? I die with impatience.

TONY: Left them? Why where should I leave them, but where I found them.

HASTINGS: This is a riddle.

TONY: Riddle me this then. What's that goes round the house, and round the house, and never touches the house?

HASTINGS: I'm still astray.

TONY: Why, that's it, mon. I have led them astray . . .

On the whole, the speeches are short, rarely running beyond a few short sentences. This gives the play its naturalness, its convincing conversation. The movement of characters off and onto the stage is also natural, because there is a reason for each movement, and the tension is kept up by the variety of situations. Goldsmith is thus able to keep together the play's different comic strains, such as the changing and developing relationships between Marlow and Kate, between Tony and the young men, and between Constance and Mrs Hardcastle. By not concentrating too long on any one aspect of the plot he contrives to give it a unity within the larger idea, the practical joke of the supposed inn.

The achievement

What Goldsmith achieved was a mixture of comic wit and farcical situation. He liked anti-climax; the absurd appealed to him. He wrote the play to amuse. There is no deep psychological profundity to be plumbed in it, no pompous posturing about problems of social relevance. So Goldsmith created a funny play, a comedy; he wrote it to give enjoyment, and in doing so he captured the comic idea of pruning excesses and captured, as well, his audience's pleasure – a thing the play has gone on doing for over two hundred years.

Part 4

Hints for study

(1) **Read the play through quickly**, marking or noting down anything you don't understand, but read it primarily to see how the mistakes of a night are entered into, how they are discovered and how they are remedied.

(2) **Then read it slowly**, making sure you understand the meaning of what the characters say. You shouldn't find this very difficult; there are not very many contemporary allusions, words or phrases which will puzzle you. (This is another reason why the play is still liked by audiences; they aren't presented with material which is difficult to understand).

(3) **Now ask yourself** where Goldsmith's skill as a dramatist is particularly to be noticed. You might consider his abilities under such headings as plot, characters, situation, and dialogue.

(a) When you are analysing the plot it will help you to make a quick summary for yourself of what happens in each act, asking yourself what Goldsmith has achieved in it. For instance, the first act tells us about the apparent nature of the characters, the last act resolves the problems, the situations into which the young characters have got themselves. You might consider how the different stories progress by following the appearances of Constance and Hastings through the play, or by tracing Marlow's meetings with Mr Hardcastle, and his meetings with Kate.

(b) When you are considering the characters it will help you to follow one character through the play. If, for instance, you decide to work on Tony first of all, you will watch how Goldsmith shows him to us on the stage – then you will collect other characters' attitudes to him. For instance, Mr Hardcastle's views of him in Act I Scene I differ from those of the landlord in Act I Scene II. You can ask yourself how Constance regards him at different parts of the play.

You will need to make up your own mind about the nature of the characters. What do you think of Mrs Hardcastle? Do you think she is punished in the last act for her earlier behaviour? Should Constance have deceived her earlier? What is your view of Marlow? Does he change? Does he perhaps need to be made a fool of? Do you think Kate was right in her estimate of him?

It will help you to collect remarks which you can quote (or to make notes about passages to which you can refer) to show these characters' natures. For instance, Marlow's remark to Hastings in Act II Scene I is a key one for anyone explaining the unusual personality:

I don't know that I was ever familiarly acquainted with a single modest woman – except my mother. But among females of another class you know –

Or, you might look closely at the passage where Mr Hardcastle keeps repeating himself in the manner of the true bore:

HARDCASTLE: Your talking of a retreat, Mr Marlow, puts me in mind of the Duke of Marlborough when we went to besiege Denain. He first summoned the garrison.

MARLOW: Don't you think the *ventre d'or* waistcoat will do with the plain brown?

HARDCASTLE: He first summoned the garrison, which might consist of about five thousand men –

HASTINGS: I think not: Brown and yellow mix but very poorly.

HARDCASTLE: I say, gentlemen, as I was telling you, he summoned the garrison, which might consist of about five thousand men –

MARLOW: The girls like finery.

HARDCASTLE: Which might consist of about five thousand men, well appointed with stones, ammunition, and other implements of war . . .

Here Mr Hardcastle is trying to break into the conversation of the two young men, without success. But he will not be deflected from the line of his anecdote, which is obviously one he tells frequently in the same way. (Remember how Diggory has earlier told of one of his stories they have laughed at for twenty years). The irony here is that Hardcastle has just told Marlow and Hastings to be under no constraint in his house: 'This is Liberty-hall, gentlemen'. They can, he says, do just as they please. They do; and thinking they are in an inn, they would naturally expect to do as they pleased, since they are paying for its service. Marlow interrupts Hardcastle's speech about the siege, and asks for a glass of punch, saying it will help them to carry on the siege with vigour, reminding him of his earlier remark about Liberty-hall.

You will see how Mrs Hardcastle begins by grumbling to Mr Hardcastle and complains about Tony's behaviour in Act I, Scene I, and continues to complain to Tony in Act II, Scene I, becoming irate with him in Act III, Scene I, where he pretends to misunderstand about the jewels. When she thinks Constance and Tony are attracted to each other in Act IV, Scene I, she becomes more amiable – briefly – to Constance: 'The jewels, my dear Con, shall be yours incontinently. You shall have them'. Notice that here she calls her Con, as she has earlier in the back to back episode (Act II, Scene I) whereas she is Constance in Act III Scene I, where Constance has asked for her jewels. She calls her 'Madam' in Act IV Scene I in her rage at reading Hasting's letter to Tony, calling to her finally as 'Miss Neville. Constance, why Constance, I say' in a most formal way. And though she shows her concern for Tony in Act V, Scene II, when she fears that a highwayman is approaching, she goes off stage in a rage. (Have you noticed how often Goldsmith gets Mrs Hardcastle and Tony offstage together, he hauling her off or she pursuing him in a rage?). And her next remarks in Act V, Scene III, are cold and ironic when she remarks that Constance and Hastings have gone: 'My dutiful niece and her gentleman, Mr Hastings'. She is determined to keep the jewels; and so she is worried when they return so quickly. Her remarks in this scene all have a touch of bitterness about them, her final one recording her disappointment in Tony: 'My undutiful off-spring'.

(c) You should consider what makes a situation comic. In *She Stoops to Conquer* the main situations largely result from mistaken identity, such as Marlow and Hastings mistaking Mr Hardcastle for an innkeeper, Marlow mistaking Kate for a barmaid. But there are failures to understand the nature of a situation, such as Marlow's giving the jewels to Mrs Hardcastle to keep, and Mrs Hardcastle's thinking she is on Crackskull Common when she is in the back of her own garden. And there are deliberate failures to understand what other people are saying, such as Tony's deliberate failure to take his mother seriously when she announces the stealing of Constance's jewels.

(d) When you study the dialogue see how Goldsmith manages to keep it flowing so that it seems natural, and clear. He uses the kind of repetition you hear in conversation, where a speaker takes up another's words. For instance, Hardcastle and Tony repeat the phrase 'of age' and the word 'refuse' in the following passage:

HARDCASTLE: . . . Come hither, Tony boy. Do you refuse this lady's hand whom I now offer you?

TONY: What signifies my refusing. You know I can't refuse her till I'm of age, father.

HARDCASTLE: While I thought concealing your age, boy, was likely to conduce to your improvement, I concurred with your mother's desire to keep it secret. But since I find she turns it to a wrong use, I must now declare, you have been of age these three months.

TONY: Of age! Am I of age, father?

HARDCASTLE: Above three months.

TONY: Then you'll see the first use I'll make of my liberty *(taking Miss Neville's hand)* Witness all men by these presents, that I, Anthony Lumpkin, Esquire, of BLANK place, refuse you Constance Neville, spinster of no place at all, for my true and lawful wife . . .

Another thing to notice in the dialogue is how Goldsmith varies it, not only in the different ways the characters talk, but also in the use he makes of long and short sentences, as well as in his use of questions and exclamation marks.

(4) **When revising** you should re-read your notes, and test whether they help you to recreate the play's events and speeches in your mind. Reading and re-reading a play never completely matches seeing it on the stage, for which it was intended. If you can, try to see *She Stoops to Conquer* performed. If you can't see it, try reading it aloud with others, or try acting it with them. This will make you envisage it on the stage and this experience will suggest questions to you: If you were producing it where would you place the characters on stage? How will they be dressed? (There are some hints in the text; can you remember them?) How will they speak? (Slowly, quickly, seriously, flippantly, aggressively, ironically and so on). Will you need to have many props, that is, items for the characters to use on stage?

(5) **When answering examination questions**, read the question paper slowly and carefully and decide which questions you can answer best. Allocate the time you will spend on each question, and be certain that you are completely clear about what the question is asking you to do. Five minutes spent considering the paper and the questions you will answer is time very well spent. You should plan your answer to each question before you begin writing it. In this way you won't forget some point and you will arrange your material coherently, giving quotations or references to the text to support your argument. Examiners do not want you to tell them things which are not relevant to the question, so make sure that you use your knowledge of the play in the right way. When you give examples which support your ideas you don't need

to quote if you can't remember accurately, but in that case you need to refer to the part of the play where you found your examples. For instance, you could simply allude to the passage in Act I Scene I where Tony tells his mother he is going to the Three Pigeons, and the kind of people he meets there. (You don't need to remember 'Dick Muggins the exciseman, Jack Slang the horse doctor, Little Aminadab that grinds the music box, and Tom Twist that spins the pewter platter' – though it is possible that the names and descriptions may have remained in your mind).

When you have finished the questions, *re-read* your answers in case you have not noticed an awkward sentence, or a word spelt wrongly, or you have not made a point clearly. Leave about five minutes for this final re-reading when you are planning how you will use your time during the examination. Remember that the examiner will have a lot of answers to read and will appreciate clear handwriting.

(6) **Questions** such as these might be set by some examiners. Before you read them, see if you can think of some questions yourself. How would *you* test someone's knowledge and understanding of the play?

(i)   Why do you think Tony misdirected Marlow and Hastings to his father's house?

(ii) Why do Mr Hardcastle and his daughter have different ideas about Marlow's character?

(iii) Do you think Tony's character changes during the play?

(iv) What kind of man is Mr Hardcastle?

(v)   Does the play give an idea of country life in the eighteenth century?

(vi) What do you think the play tells you about the arrangement of marriages in the eighteenth century?

(vii) What conclusions do you draw about Marlow and Hastings from their appearance in *The Three Pigeons* and their first meeting with Mr Hardcastle?

(viii) If you were producing the play what scenery would you need? And what stage properties? Prove your points by referring to the text.

(ix) Do you see any differences between Kate and Constance?

(x)   What is your view of Marlow's character?

(xi) How is Mrs Hardcastle's character illustrated?

(xii) Show how some of the play's stock comic devices – such as the reading aloud of Tony's letter or the use of the screen – are used to show a character in a different light, or to alter a situation.

(7) **Sample answers** are not to be taken as necessarily correct or ideal. What matters is *your* reaction to the play, *your* ideas about it, *your*

ability to show that you understand it and appreciate the skill of its author. The following sample answers are merely meant as a guide, an example of how the writer of these Notes would answer the questions.

QUESTION: *Do you see any differences between Kate and Constance?*

A SUGGESTED ANSWER: Kate and Constance are in different situations. Constance wants to marry Hastings; before he died, her father approved of him. She conceals these facts from Mrs Hardcastle, her guardian, because Mrs Hardcastle wants her to marry Tony. Kate, on the other hand, begins the play fancy-free. She and her father speak freely to each other once he has told her that he intends her to marry Marlow, though he says he will not control her choice. Here he differs from his wife, who is trying to compel Tony and Constance to marry. Both Constance and Kate indulge in some deception. Constance does this because she wants to keep her fortune and marry Hastings when she is of age. Kate deceives Marlow because she wants to find out what kind of a man he is.

Kate is successful in persuading her father to give her time to prove to him that Marlow is not the kind of man he thinks he is. Kate does not deceive her father. Constance, however, pretends to love Tony in order to deceive Mrs Hardcastle. She fails, however, to get her jewels by asking Mrs Hardcastle for them. And she fails to keep Hastings's letter from Mrs Hardcastle.

Kate, having won time, proves her point to her father and Sir Charles by leading Marlow into speaking confidently to her in front of the screen. And she is in a position to forgive him for his mistaking her for a poor relation.

Constance, however, has apparently lost both her jewels and the chance to run away with Hastings. Were it not for Tony's stratagem she would have had to wait three years, probably in the care of her stern Aunt Pedigree, before she could marry Hastings.

Constance has not had to act a part to find out Hastings's nature, or to learn his love; her problems have been to escape from Mrs Hardcastle's treatment of her, to marry the man she loves and to retain her fortune. Kate has to discover whether she loves Marlow, and, if so, whether he will care enough for her to want to marry her for herself, not knowing that she is, in fact, the girl of whom his father approves and is well to do. Kate has also to persuade both fathers of the true nature of Marlow's character, and that they should marry each other.

Kate enjoys flirting with and teasing Marlow, Constance and Hastings are settled in their regard for each other. Kate – as barmaid and then as poor relation – stoops to conquer her hero; Constance, as she says, has had to 'stoop to dissimulation' to avoid oppression and, ultimately, to be able to marry Hastings and keep her fortune. And so their roles have been different, though they have led to the happiness each girl gains at the end of the play.

QUESTION: *What conclusions do you draw about Marlow and Hastings from their appearance in* The Three Pigeons *and their first meeting with Mr Hardcastle?*

A SUGGESTED ANSWER: Marlow and Hastings seem strange to the country people in *The Three Pigeons*. The landlord says they look like Frenchmen. They have not asked their way because Marlow is so reserved. Hastings asks the way, and Marlow shows some irritation at Tony's roundabout teasing answers. He doesn't like Tony's facetiousness. Neither Marlow nor Hastings likes discomfort.

Before they meet Mr Hardcastle, the first thing they remark on when they enter Mr Hardcastle's house is its warmth and cleanliness. Then Marlow's wide experience of inns, and his travelling are made clear, as well as the result of this way of living, his shyness in the presence of women of reputation, and his readiness to say fine things to barmaids and servants. We are told that he is terrified of meeting the lady his father would like him to marry; that he has come down to help Hastings to introduce him as his friend to Miss Neville's family. We hear Marlow has a stammer and doesn't think much of his own appearance.

This makes a contrast when we see his assurance with Mr Hardcastle. Marlow and Hastings discuss what they'll wear. They are concerned about their appearance, and obviously have a lot of clothes with them.

When Hardcastle goes on talking Marlow is peremptory with him at first, demanding a glass of punch. When the punch comes he decides to humour Hardcastle, thinking him a character. However, once Hardcastle begins to bore them again, Marlow demands to know what is for supper, and asks for the cook to be called. Then Hastings demands the bill of fare and remarks on Hardcastle's giving himself airs, 'All upon the high ropes! His uncle a colonel! . . .' Both young men are at first contemptuous of the rich meal, and demand plain fare, then Marlow says that Hardcastle can send them what he pleases, and, despite Hardcastle's saying it's unnecessary, insists on seeing the beds are properly aired.

Marlow and Hastings are obviously well-dressed young men, sure of themselves in many respects despite Marlow's reserve and the shyness we hear he has with ladies. They are accustomed to getting their own way and know what they want. They have found the travel fatiguing and seem unused to the country. While they are peremptory with Hardcastle they regard him as a character, though an innkeeper, and are unaware he regards them as full of impudence while treating them as his guests.

Part 5

Suggestions for further reading

The text

The play has been frequently re-printed. A convenient contemporary edition is
She Stoops to Conquer, edited by A. Norman Jeffares, Macmillan, London. 1965.

Other works by Goldsmith

The Works, 5 volumes, edited by Arthur Friedman, Clarendon Press, Oxford, 1966. The standard edition, well annotated; there are other editions of Goldsmith's *Works* but this is by far the most useful.
Selected Works, edited by R. Garnett (Reynard Library) Hart-Davis, London, 1950. This contains a good selection of Goldsmith's writings.
A Goldsmith Selection, edited by A. Norman Jeffares, Macmillan, London, 1963. A shorter book than the Reynard Libary Edition, containing poems, essays and letters.

Criticism and biography

GINGER, JOHN: *The Notable Man,* Hamish Hamilton, London, 1977. The best biography.
GWYNN, STEPHEN: *Oliver Goldsmith,* Thornton Butterworth, London, 1935. Gwynn wrote this biography with insight and sympathy; it also contains many well-selected quotations from Goldsmith's writing.
HILLES, F.W.(ED.): *Portraits by Sir Joshua Reynolds,* in *The Private Papers of James Boswell,* Volume III, Yale University Press, New Haven, Connecticut, 1952. This contains a life by Goldsmith's friend Reynolds which is the most understanding contemporary view of his character.
JEFFARES, A. NORMAN: *Oliver Goldsmith* (in *Writers and Their Work* series) Longmans (for the British Council), London, 1959; revised ed., 1965.
LUCAS, F.L.: *The Search for Good Sense: Four eighteenth century characters,* Cassell, London, 1958. This has a sensible discussion of Goldsmith.

The author of these notes

A. NORMAN JEFFARES was educated at the Universities of Dublin and Oxford. He taught classics at Trinity College, Dublin, was Lector in English at Groningen University, Lecturer in English Literature at the University of Edinburgh, Jury Professor of English Language and Literature at the University of Adelaide, Professor of English Literature at the University of Leeds and is now Professor of English at the University of Stirling. He has written books on and edited writings by Anglo-Irish writers (Swift, Farquhar, Goldsmith, Sheridan, Maria Edgeworth, George Moore, and W.B. Yeats) and he has edited works by Congreve, Cowper and Whitman. At present he is writing a *History of Anglo-Irish Literature*. He is Chairman of the Literature Committee of the Scottish Arts Council.

York Notes: list of titles

CHINUA ACHEBE
Things Fall Apart

EDWARD ALBEE
Who's Afraid of Virginia Woolf?

MARGARET ATWOOD
Cat's Eye
The Handmaid's Tale

W. H. AUDEN
Selected Poems

JANE AUSTEN
Emma
Mansfield Park
Northanger Abbey
Persuasion
Pride and Prejudice
Sense and Sensibility

SAMUEL BECKETT
Waiting for Godot

ALAN BENNETT
Talking Heads

ARNOLD BENNETT
The Card

JOHN BETJEMAN
Selected Poems

WILLIAM BLAKE
Songs of Innocence, Songs of Experience

ROBERT BOLT
A Man For All Seasons

CHARLOTTE BRONTË
Jane Eyre

EMILY BRONTË
Wuthering Heights

ROBERT BURNS
Selected Poems

BYRON
Selected Poems

GEOFFREY CHAUCER
The Franklin's Tale
The Knight's Tale
The Merchant's Tale
The Miller's Tale
The Nun's Priest's Tale
The Pardoner's Tale
Prologue to the Canterbury Tales
The Wife of Bath's Tale

SAMUEL TAYLOR COLERIDGE
Selected Poems

JOSEPH CONRAD
Heart of Darkness

DANIEL DEFOE
Moll Flanders
Robinson Crusoe

SHELAGH DELANEY
A Taste of Honey

CHARLES DICKENS
Bleak House
David Copperfield
Great Expectations
Hard Times
Oliver Twist

EMILY DICKINSON
Selected Poems

JOHN DONNE
Selected Poems

DOUGLAS DUNN
Selected Poems

GEORGE ELIOT
Middlemarch
The Mill on the Floss
Silas Marner

T. S. ELIOT
Four Quartets
Selected Poems
The Waste Land

HENRY FIELDING
Joseph Andrews

F. SCOTT FITZGERALD
The Great Gatsby

GUSTAVE FLAUBERT
Madame Bovary

E. M. FORSTER
Howards End
A Passage to India

JOHN FOWLES
The French Lieutenant's Woman

BRIAN FRIEL
Translations

ELIZABETH GASKELL
North and South

WILLIAM GOLDING
Lord of the Flies

OLIVER GOLDSMITH
She Stoops to Conquer

GRAHAM GREENE
Brighton Rock
The Heart of the Matter
The Power and the Glory

THOMAS HARDY
Far from the Madding Crowd
Jude the Obscure
The Mayor of Casterbridge
The Return of the Native
Selected Poems
Tess of the D'Urbervilles

L. P. HARTLEY
The Go-Between

NATHANIEL HAWTHORNE
The Scarlet Letter

SEAMUS HEANEY
Selected Poems

ERNEST HEMINGWAY
A Farewell to Arms
The Old Man and the Sea

SUSAN HILL
I'm the King of the Castle

HOMER
The Iliad
The Odyssey

GERARD MANLEY HOPKINS
Selected Poems

TED HUGHES
Selected Poems

ALDOUS HUXLEY
Brave New World

HENRY JAMES
The Portrait of a Lady

BEN JONSON
The Alchemist
Volpone

JAMES JOYCE
Dubliners
A Portrait of the Artist as a Young Man

JOHN KEATS
Selected Poems

PHILIP LARKIN
Selected Poems

D. H. LAWRENCE
The Rainbow
Selected Short Stories
Sons and Lovers
Women in Love

HARPER LEE
To Kill a Mockingbird

LAURIE LEE
Cider with Rosie

CHRISTOPHER MARLOWE
Doctor Faustus

ARTHUR MILLER
The Crucible
Death of a Salesman
A View from the Bridge

JOHN MILTON
Paradise Lost I & II
Paradise Lost IV & IX

TONI MORRISON
Beloved

SEAN O'CASEY
Juno and the Paycock

GEORGE ORWELL
Animal Farm
Nineteen Eighty-four

JOHN OSBORNE
Look Back in Anger

WILFRED OWEN
Selected Poems

HAROLD PINTER
The Caretaker

SYLVIA PLATH
Selected Works

POETRY OF THE FIRST WORLD WAR

ALEXANDER POPE
Selected Poems

J. B. PRIESTLEY
An Inspector Calls

JEAN RHYS
The Wide Sargasso Sea

J. D. SALINGER
The Catcher in the Rye

WILLIAM SHAKESPEARE
Antony and Cleopatra
As You Like It
Coriolanus
Hamlet
Henry IV Part I
Henry IV Part II
Henry V
Julius Caesar
King Lear
Macbeth
Measure for Measure
The Merchant of Venice
A Midsummer Night's Dream
Much Ado About Nothing
Othello
Richard II
Richard III
Romeo and Juliet
Sonnets
The Taming of the Shrew
The Tempest
Twelfth Night
The Winter's Tale

GEORGE BERNARD SHAW
Arms and the Man
Pygmalion
Saint Joan

MARY SHELLEY
Frankenstein

RICHARD BRINSLEY SHERIDAN
The Rivals

R. C. SHERRIFF
Journey's End

MURIEL SPARK
The Prime of Miss Jean Brodie

JOHN STEINBECK
The Grapes of Wrath
Of Mice and Men
The Pearl

TOM STOPPARD
Rosencrantz and Guildenstern are Dead

JONATHAN SWIFT
Gulliver's Travels

JOHN MILLINGTON SYNGE
The Playboy of the Western World

MILDRED D. TAYLOR
Roll of Thunder, Hear My Cry

W. M. THACKERAY
Vanity Fair

MARK TWAIN
Huckleberry Finn

VIRGIL
The Aeneid

DEREK WALCOTT
Selected Poems

ALICE WALKER
The Color Purple

JOHN WEBSTER
The Duchess of Malfi

OSCAR WILDE
The Importance of Being Earnest

TENNESSEE WILLIAMS
Cat on a Hot Tin Roof
A Streetcar Named Desire

VIRGINIA WOOLF
Mrs Dalloway
To the Lighthouse

WILLIAM WORDSWORTH
Selected Poems

W. B. YEATS
Selected Poems

York Handbooks: list of titles

YORK HANDBOOKS form a companion series to York Notes and are designed to meet the wider needs of students of English and related fields. Each volume is a compact study of a given subject area, written by an authority with experience in communicating the essential ideas to students at all levels.

AN A.B.C. OF SHAKESPEARE
by P. C. BAYLEY

A DICTIONARY OF BRITISH AND IRISH AUTHORS
by ANTONY KAMM

A DICTIONARY OF LITERARY TERMS (Second Edition)
by MARTIN GRAY

ENGLISH POETRY
by CLIVE T. PROBYN

AN INTRODUCTION TO AUSTRALIAN LITERATURE
by TREVOR JAMES

AN INTRODUCTION TO LINGUISTICS
by LORETO TODD

AN INTRODUCTORY GUIDE TO ENGLISH LITERATURE
by MARTIN STEPHEN

STUDYING CHAUCER
by ELISABETH BREWER

STUDYING JANE AUSTEN
by IAN MILLIGAN

STUDYING SHAKESPEARE
by MARTIN STEPHEN *and* PHILIP FRANKS

WOMEN WRITERS IN ENGLISH LITERATURE
by JANE STEVENSON